# Leader
# Relativity

# ADVANCED PRAISE FOR LEADER RELATIVITY

*"Finally someone that gets what new leaders are going through. Having read countless books on the subject I can say with certainty, this book is unlike anything else out there. Leader Relativity is a completely fresh take on the subject, and I would highly recommend this book to anyone who is interested in a career in leadership, but unsure where to start."*

- Aaron Rothlisberger, Radio Frequency Engineer

*"Throughout the book it really felt like Joe was coaching me one-on-one through the process, which is exactly what I needed. His plain-english style of writing immediately connected with me, and is probably why I couldn't seem to put it down. Engaging, insightful, and often humorous, Leader Relativity is everything you'd hope it to be, and absolutely belongs on your bookshelf."*

- Eric Hoffman, ICU Registered Nurse

*"Joe has an uncanny ability to put himself in the shoes of new leaders, understand what they are going through, and then give them all the tools and information required to actually become leaders in the real world. This book is a refreshing example of what it means to lead by example, and should be required reading for anyone considering a career in management, period."*

- Elizabeth Naglak, Head Baker

*"Take everything you know about leadership, and toss it out the window. I can only hope that our next generation of leaders finds this book. Not only for their sake, but for ours too."*

- Danielle Achziger, Vice President of Client Solutions

*"Whether you've been leading teams for three decades or three days, there is something in here for you. Thought-provoking and easy to digest, it's immediately evident the passion Joe has for the subject. I challenge anyone to walk away from this book without a deeper understanding of what leadership is."*

- Kris Peterson, Escalation Associate

# Leader Relativity

## Joe Reichert

JOURNEY INK PUBLISHING - COLORADO

Journey Ink Publishing
An imprint of Journey Institute Press,
a division of 50 in 52 Journey, Inc.
journeyinstitutepress.org

Library of Congress Control Number: 2023944212
Names: Reichert, Joe
Title: Leader Relativity
Description: Colorado: Journey Ink Publishing, 2023
Identifiers: ISBN 979-8-9875066-9-1 (hardcover)
978-1-964754-06-2 (paperback)
979-8-9886470-6-5 (ebook/kindle)
Subjects: BISAC: BUSINESS & ECONOMICS / Leadership |
BUSINESS & ECONOMICS / Management |
BUSINESS & ECONOMICS / Skills

First Edition

Printed in the United States of America

1 2 3 4 5 23 24 25 26 27

This book was typeset in Acme Gothic / Addington CF

Editing by: Jessica Medberry - InkWhale Editorial LLC

Dedicated to anyone who has ever been told you don't have what it takes to be a leader.

They're wrong.

You do.

And I'm about to prove it.

# Contents

# Introduction

I've got a secret that I'm dying to tell. What I teach in this book—how to become a leader that others actually want to follow—goes against the last sixty years of leadership development. At work I'm a pariah, an outcast, for teaching this style of leadership. And it's not because I actively choose to ignore the rules. No, it's far scarier than that. It's because this actually works, and it scares the crap out of our corporate suits that anyone in our company—regardless of their job title, years of experience, or the amount of power they have—can become an extraordinary leader at any moment.

For ages, becoming a leader has been seen as overly complicated and therefore a large undertaking, which is exactly what I set out to dispel with this book. And as you can clearly tell by holding it in your hands, it isn't that long because, to be frank, it doesn't need to be. Leadership, at its core, isn't all that complex. If someone told me it would take four hundred–plus pages to describe how to become a carpenter, I'd be a little worried that woodworking might not be for me.

I had just one goal in mind for writing this: to help you on your journey toward becoming an incredible leader. That's it—that's all I want. An exceptional leader. The type we all deserve, and the one that people will expect you to be for them. I truly believe that anyone on earth can become a leader once they know the basics behind how leadership works. So, for the next two hundred pages, I'm going to coach you and guide you through your first steps into leadership as best I can (the way I wish someone had done for me). However, I am not going to promise you that this transformation will be easy, or that by the end of this book you will even be a leader. That's just not how books work, and certainly not how leadership does. The people who sell you that falsehood are manipulating you—and as such—giant turds.

So, let's be real from the start. I'm not here to get rich. I didn't write this so I could add it to my LinkedIn. And I don't have social media because it's stupid, so becoming famous or gaining Twitter followers isn't on my radar. I did this for you (which was me eight years ago), someone just starting out on their leadership path and a bit put off at how overwhelming becoming a leader seems.

When I made the choice to become a leader, I was hopelessly lost. I knew I liked helping people and being a part of teams, so I did what most do: I started watching YouTube and reading books on leadership. I read a ton of bestsellers and watched the most popular TED Talks around. Most of them were pretty good—great, in fact. The problem was that the more I read and watched, the more confused I became.

Leadership teachers and coaches have been trending in the right direction for a while now, slowly breaking free from the antiquated versions of leadership our grandparents knew. But read one book, then another, and you'll probably have two very different ideas on the subject. Both equally useful, but how they are related to each other, and more importantly, how to actually become the leader they are describing—seemingly one of life's great mysteries. I realized that we're missing an absolute basic primer on leadership. A first book to turn to on the subject when you're a newborn, giant-headed leadership baby. Not something that describes traits of modern leaders, not more made-up "leadership laws" that we all have to remember and live by. Just bare-bones, down-to-its-core leadership. So, I set out to give people like you just that. The one thing I wish I would've had when I first started. And I made a promise to myself when I began writing: keep it real.

For the love of all things holy, Joe, please don't sell out.

Don't write it based on what you think a publisher will like or what people at work will think. Screw 'em. Write it how you think it will best resonate with someone. If you're moved to swear, then swear. If you have to talk a little sh*t, so be it. Just write it like something you would've actually wanted to read. And as long as someone out there is consuming this, in any way, shape, or form—I will have done my job. All I care about is helping people become better leaders.

This is how I actually talk.

This is how I would speak if we met in real life.

That's how I wrote the book.

You don't know it yet, but people you have never met will one day need you to be a great leader. And you now owe it to them to be that person.

# Chapter 1
## The Sweats

I must've looked like an idiot. My stomach was tight, and I was probably (definitely) sweating. Pushing my discount deodorant well past its limit, I opened my mouth and squeaked out what might be the least confident sentence of my entire life: "Hey guys, I'm Joe, and I'm your new head coach." Damn, I was four seconds into being a leader and it definitely wasn't going well. In that moment I was supposed to be the epitome of confidence, proving to the team (and hopefully myself too) that I was the new head honcho—the one to lead us to victory and, in the process, have all the answers. In reality, I had no idea what I was doing, I was terrified, and it probably (definitely) showed.

The rest of that first practice is a blur. I went on to survive day one, but as I drove home, I couldn't stop spiraling. "Well, that sucked. Maybe I'm just not cut out to be a leader . . . At least they didn't mutiny." And if I knew it wouldn't make me vomit, I'd love to rewatch that interaction again. I'm sure my voice cracked (at the ripe age of twenty-seven), my knees uncontrollably shaking like a newborn giraffe's.

Looking back, I have just one overarching theme from that year: I was not ready to be a leader. It's not that I wasn't up for the challenge of coaching a semiprofessional rugby team, but rather that my leadership preparation had not done its job. You see, for months leading up to that moment, I had read and listened to all the classics on how to lead other humans. The laws of leadership, the theories, the examples—you name it and I had consumed it. A giant abstract painting in my head with random tidbits splattered all over.

I knew the buzzwords and I could list off the traits of great modern leaders. I could stand toe to toe with just about anyone and rattle off popular TED Talks and leadership books. Yet, for whatever reason (I know it now, I didn't then), I was fundamentally unprepared to be a leader. Jumping-out-of-a-plane-with-no-parachute unprepared. But it wasn't my fault. And I want to be clear—if you feel this way right now, it isn't your fault either.

*** 

As you'll soon learn, I am in no way a stoic person. I like to joke around—dare I say be silly—at times. Making someone laugh is one of my favorite things on earth. But I knew, or I mistakenly "knew," that leaders who are after results don't really kid around. I mean, how could they? *(Curmudgeonly furrows brow.)* "The job of a leader is to drive their team to success." Make a plan, execute said plan, win or achieve desired results. Classic leaders come to mind in this traditional context. The type of people you see on money, or who have statues made of them. Not folks you'd want to grab a beer with, but successful, winning leaders nonetheless.

But hold up, because this is where things went off the rails for me.

Hadn't I also read that modern leaders are compassionate, authentic, and vulnerable? The type of stuff that Brené Brown and Simon Sinek, two leadership geniuses, have been preaching now for years? That extending empathy and kindness are actually signs of great leadership? So, which is it? Because a leader can't possibly be both, leading their team to victory while also being a normal human.

Or maybe they can, but only if that person knows the perfect mixture of the two. The elusive point where you're still taken seriously as the boss, but just enough personality is allowed to peek through so you don't come off as a robot.

That first year of coaching, I tried all the combinations, and I failed every way you can imagine. I thought maybe 60/40 was the right blend of modern leader traits with traditional leader responsibilities. Our team lost a bunch of games, so clearly that wasn't it. Then I thought, maybe it's actually closer to 50/50? Because surely it can't be 80/20 (now that's just ridiculous). Needless to say, the result was a confusing mess, and it turned me into someone I wasn't. Someone I thought I needed to be, and for way too long.

Spoiler alert—it didn't work. Not only did it feel weird, but the team didn't win many games, which made me realize that trying to find some magical balance between being authoritative and compassionate can't be the solution. Eventually, after years of struggling through what leadership actually is, I started to get things right. Then one day I was hit by a semitruck of a thought: I can't possibly be the only one who has struggled with this. Which is why right now, on this very page, I want to take a moment to commend you for even picking up a book on leadership.

✳✳✳

Can we be real for a second? The place you're at right now in your leadership journey can seem pretty overwhelming at times (all times). In fact, speaking from personal experience, it can be downright scary when you make the decision to become a leader. How I usually describe it to people is "Oh sh*t, what the f*ck am I doing?" mixed with a light touch of food poisoning. Upset stomach, body sweats at 3:00 a.m., and constant regret are, unfortunately, all hallmarks of this stage.

So, I first want to reassure you: what you're feeling is normal.

Disturbingly normal, in fact. Every leader there has ever been, the very best you can think of, all felt this same self-doubt and fear when they first started. "Really Joe? People like Maya Angelou and Gandhi had sweaty armpits too?" Yep. It may not have lasted long, and most people nowadays will never admit it since doing so is seen as a faux pas, but I've candidly spoken to enough leaders that I'm comfortable making this statement with complete confidence: every leader there has ever been has felt this new-leader shock. And believe it or not, as I'm about to show you, I actually think it's harder now than it's ever been to become a leader.

# Chapter 2
## Source of Confusion

Pop quiz: Which of these is not pizza?

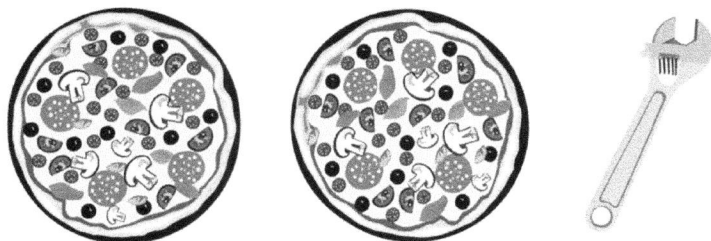

Well done. Insanely simple, yes, but what was the thought process that went on inside your head? As humans, we're pretty good at comparing objects (is this thing like the other things?). In fact, we oddly enjoy it. *I Spy* and *Where's Waldo?* were classics in our house growing up. For the case above, you just knew at a glance which one wasn't correct. Circular with toppings and crust, pizza is ingrained in our heads. The silhouette of a wrench is rarely mistaken for one.

But you also know what pizza is, which is a fundamentally different kind of knowledge. The ingredients, the smell, the way it should burn your mouth like lava on first bite. It's with this understanding of the usual characteristics that you could go deeper than just a visual comparison. For instance, if I handed you a prop pizza made from plastic, you would tell me that this stiff disk, although shaped and colored like a pizza, is not indeed an edible pie. So, how does one acquire this knowledge? Well, like most of planet Earth, we've been exposed to pizza. Smelled it. Tasted it. Stuffed it in a microwave the morning after a long night out. We know pizza.

Now let's say you meet someone who has never had that cheesy, doughy, saucy goodness—could you describe to them what goes into one so they don't get tricked into thinking something else is a pizza? Is there a formula you could give them to ensure they aren't tricked by a wrench, or its second cousin, the hammer?

*** 

If I showed you a picture of someone, could you tell me whether they were a leader? Is it even possible to spot one with the naked eye? The answer is a resounding *no*. It's much more difficult to pick out leaders than pizzas. There is no standard silhouette of a great leader (besides humanoid). You have to get to know someone first, to understand who they are and how they treat other people, to determine this. But to even start this exercise, we need to know what a leader actually is. We need something to compare them against.

I'd like you to think of a great leader you've had in the past. Someone that really sticks out above the rest. Now, try to describe what made them such a great leader to you. Was it how they blew their whistle or managed the budget? The way they delegated tasks or submitted reports? I doubt it. Functional tasks like those are almost never on the list. If you're having trouble conjuring up an answer, let me give you a nudge: How did that person make you *feel* when you were around them?

A while ago, I developed a simple one-question test to help me determine whether someone was indeed a leader: *Would I inconvenience myself for them?* Not necessarily an end state to be working toward, but I realized that if someone had been a leader in my life, I always ended up answering *yes* to this question. Applied in a work setting, would I stay late to support them in achieving one of their goals? For those I regarded as leaders in the past (sometimes it was a coworker, sometimes it was my actual boss), this choice was a no-brainer; they simply needed to ask and I would've done it. I may not have lit up at the idea, but it mattered to me that they accomplished their objectives. However, on the flip side, I have absolutely had managers that I consider to be horrible leaders, and in every case, I would've gladly opted for a root canal instead.

Why should I stay late for someone when I know with absolute certainty that they wouldn't do the same for me? Someone that clearly doesn't care about me as a person and only wants my help for their own personal gain? Now yes, sometimes we have to stay late because it's part of our job, but take a temperature reading the next time you're doing it. If you feel like this is a hypocritical injustice—that person is probably a bad leader, and I have yet to meet someone that breaks this rule.

But what are the actual ingredients that make someone a good leader versus a bad leader? This test is a great short-cut, but it glosses over all the nuance involved in leadership. It can also double as a test to tell you whether someone is a jerk, which is not its intended purpose. Telling you to simply *be someone others would stay late for* is a recipe for disaster. That's not leadership. We need a standard for identifying the good versus the bad leadership ingredients. A rubric that will tell us what is—and is not—a leader. It's an exercise eerily similar to describing an orange.

\*\*\*

Describe the word orange. For starters, did you pick a noun or an adjective? Orange is an unmistakable color, but it's also a citrus fruit whose slices belong in summer beverages. Now, say you picked the fruit version. How would you describe its color? "Oranges are . . . orange?" Uh-oh, it's always trouble when a definition has the word in it. You might then tell me, "You just know an orange when you see it," to which I would agree and counter with "But how would you teach someone else how to identify an orange if they've never seen one before?"

"A spherical citrus fruit that grows on trees?"

Not quite.

"It's rounder and well . . . orange." *(Facepalm.)* This deceivingly difficult exercise is a lot like defining leadership, as the definition usually has the word *leader* sprinkled somewhere in it. It's also tricky to nail down because of the many forms the word can take: a noun (a leader), a verb (leading), or even an adjective (lead detective). This is part of what makes learning about leadership so difficult in the beginning. Without context, it's hard to tell whether I'm learning how to grow an orange, peel an orange, make a drink, describe a sunset, or identify a chewed crayon.

And the confusion is only compounded by how the word *leader* is used today. As a manager, I constantly get emails at work that start with the greeting "Hello Leaders . . ." when in reality there are names on the "TO:" line that I absolutely don't consider good leaders. Managers with functional authority, yes, but individuals who I have heard say deplorable things to employees. Individuals who abuse the system and consistently put their own needs ahead of those on their team. And yet there they are on these emails, being addressed as a leader. Which ultimately sends a weird message—no matter how you behave, you can still be a leader—and that is entirely incorrect. We've convoluted the word, and the result is a colossal mess.

# Chapter 3
## Lost

"Hey Katie, congratulations on finishing up your leadership program, that's quite an achievement! So, I have to know, after three years studying the subject, how has your view on leadership changed since before you started the program? What does leadership mean to you now?"

No answer, complete silence.

I could see the smoke start to pour out of her head as her brain imploded. Trying in vain to recall which seminar or networking event had prepared her for this question, she politely told me she was in a rush (she was now clearly flustered) and that she would get back to me. The next day I got an email from her that was over eight hundred words long. Verbose, thorough, and most of which I agreed with. Though as I read it, I couldn't help but wonder—does it really take all of *this* to describe what leadership is? Is this topic just fundamentally that complicated?

In fact, if you're up for it, I'll challenge you to answer the same question right now: *What is leadership?* Little did I know that just about everyone involved with the subject (teaching it, practicing it, coaching it) struggles to find an answer. Since then, I've asked a lot of people *What is leadership?*—including some very high-up and experienced leaders—and the most popular response by far is stunned silence. Often followed by "Now that's a good question" and finally a few minutes of examples and comparisons. Pretty good stuff in general, but I had to know: Is leadership really this difficult to pin down?

My entire life I've heard the reassuring phrase "Anyone can become a leader." However, from what I was seeing and hearing, I wasn't quite sure that was true. How could it be, when conveying it to someone else appeared to be impossible? How could one person encompass all those different (sometimes drastically different) definitions? It just wasn't feasible. So, I came to this conclusion: either leadership is much simpler than we are making it, or it is so difficult that becoming one actually isn't possible for everyone (and I refused to accept option B).

***

There are more theories, resources, and viral videos on leadership than ever before. Which is why compiling them on your own into a cohesive reference to work toward is so insanely difficult, and this unfortunately turns a lot of folks away. The laws of leadership, servant leadership, transformational leadership, extreme ownership, vulnerable leadership, the golden circle, etc., etc., etc. They're great (amazing even), but it's a lot.

The first thought I had when I tried to ingest all those modern resources was "But how do I actually go out and do all those things?" How does one become *that?* And if you've had that same thought, we might've shared this one too: "Okay, then I'll just search out what leadership is at its core, the absolute fundamentals, and start from there." Although I would commend you for this logical line of reasoning—try as you may, there are not many leadership teachers, speakers, or coaches out there talking about what leadership actually is. In fact, I've found none. Seen a lot of *Great leaders are a lot like this,* and *All the best leaders live by this simple rule, or Let me tell you this intense story that ends with me becoming a great leader.* But do enough watching, reading, or listening on the subject, and you may get the feeling that leadership at its core is just a really well-kept secret. One of life's great mysteries, like Stonehenge or why dentists try to talk to you when they know you can't respond. A seemingly simple and innocent question—*What is leadership?*—yet so absurdly difficult to answer.

And to be candid, for a long time I did not have an answer to this either. Although I had never been asked the question, I know that if put on the spot, I too would've created a tangled web of an answer, one that I eventually deemed good enough to avoid embarrassment in the moment. Like most people, I thought you just *did* leadership. Everyone knew what that meant. Or, so I thought.

It's an unfortunate reality, but there is so much non-coherent gibberish out there that, sadly, some will tap out before ever getting started. Throw in the towel. Call it quits. Decide it's easier to live a life from the middle than attempt to unravel the tangled extension cord that is leadership.

But when you label something, you take the fear out of it.

This stage of your journey is probably best described as knowing you want to go somewhere, but Google Maps refuses to work—or, back in the day, lacking directions or a compass (all ages are welcome here). In either case, you're hosed. And the most frustrating part when first starting out is that nobody teaching leadership remembers what it was like to be here in your shoes. They talk at us like great leadership is a given (which it might be for them), connecting dots quickly and making giant leaps between ideas. But like a calculus teacher who dares utter the word *easy* in class, or parents that insist on using slang—they just don't get it. They've lost touch.

You can't go somewhere new without a destination and a map. That's just science. "Meet me at Tommy's house. Take Bonnet Street and then turn right at the house that looks like a giant apple." Could be better, but it would get the job done. Now imagine a strange world where you asked me where we were meeting, and I didn't give you the location; I just told you, "You'll know it when you see it." Or I compared how to get to Tommy's with how I tell people to find my friend Amanda's house. Or better yet, I handed you a six-page MapQuest printout straight from 2003 on how to get there. These useless options can mean only one thing: you're screwed.

Even in some alternate reality where you somehow managed to find a place you deemed the correct destination, could you replicate the process? Would you know if you were off track when trying to do it again? And could you explain to someone else where to go or how to get there?

Yes, eventually, if you go somewhere enough times, you will no longer need a map. Though without one in the beginning, you may just keep going to the wrong place forever. This is what confuses and frustrates me about how leadership is being taught. How can anyone expect people like you to become amazing leaders if nobody can describe what it is? Those who hope to help others become leaders must be able to answer *What is leadership?* It's imperative. And if leadership teachers give you, an emerging and eager-to-learn leader, ten different sets of directions that take you to ten different locations, well then bless your soul—I hope you brought water.

I realized what we needed is a cheat sheet. A simplified version of leadership. A hey-no-kidding, this-is-where-you-should-definitely-start introduction to the subject. A reference created for the absolute newcomer and one that works in every scenario, is easily shared, and can be referred to quickly when required. Which brings me to this sentence in this book.

# Chapter 4
## You And I

I would be ecstatic if everyone, no matter where they are on their leadership journey, picked up and read this book. I think there are things in here that every skill set and experience level can benefit from. But to be frank, I didn't write this book for everyone.

This book has one intended audience, and if up to this point I have made you feel even a smidge more at ease, confident, understood, or just generally better about the idea of actually becoming a leader—then you are who I had in mind. And I'm in a strangely unique position to help. I'm close enough to the start of my own leadership journey that I can relate to where you are and what you're feeling, but I'm also far enough along that I've learned what works and what doesn't (painfully at times).

"So, Joe, why should I listen to you?"—an excellent question. You've probably noticed that I don't spend ten pages listing off my credentials or bragging about career accomplishments that nobody cares about. That's on purpose, because as I'm about to prove to you over and over again—they don't matter. Humans are irrational creatures. For something that tells us Krispy Kreme doughnuts at midnight are a good idea, we sure seem to trust our gut for a lot of things—especially when deciding who to take advice from. That's why we buy workout equipment at 2:00 a.m. from companies with celebrity endorsements, when in reality, a PhD in exercise science would be better suited to tell us the benefits of that overpriced piece of machinery. So, why is Shaquille O'Neal so much more compelling than Dr. Recent Yale Grad? It's because we feel like we already have a connection with him.

Shaq doesn't have an advanced degree in physiology, but we trust Shaq. He's funny. He's on the pizza commercials wearing wigs. We can picture ourselves getting a beer with Shaq and watching him awkwardly pick up regular-sized objects in his enormous hands. We've spent countless hours watching these celebrities make us laugh, cry, and cringe on TV that oddly, we already trust them.

This is why most speakers come with a five-minute introduction listing off their accomplishments before ever emitting a sound from their mouth. They want to establish that same Shaq-like trust with their audience under the incorrect assumption that a lengthy track record will make us think, "Wow, look at all the things they've done. I'm definitely going to listen to what this suit jacket has to say." The only problem is that this isn't really trust. It's like saying Pop-Tarts have fruit in them. Sure, on the surface, it's enough to start a business transaction. I speak, you listen because I am established with credentials, the end. But here's the problem: I don't want you to politely listen to me. I want you to absorb this and tuck it away deep in your cerebellum with where the Britney lyrics live. I want an *Inception*-level interaction so I can make an actual impact on your leadership journey. In fact, nothing would make me happier than if one day you are leading a meeting at work, lose your train of thought, and randomly think to yourself, "Son of a b*tch, Joe was right. Leadership really is this simple."

However, getting to the point where you trust me enough to keep reading has nothing to do with what I've done in the past (zero percent, in fact). It's enough to open the book, but getting to the finish line requires something else. That is a decision we all make with our intestines, and it's only going to happen if you and I have a connection.

\*\*\*

Building a meaningful relationship is hard enough, let alone in a book where it's just me talking to you, but here I will try my best. First and foremost, let's get one thing straight: this is who I am in real life, and I obviously don't speak like some sort of sentient leadership textbook. Whenever I hear people like that, I instantly think, "What is wrong with this person?" I have a lot of energy in real life (along with high blood pressure), and I want you to feel my passion for this subject as you're reading. I'm here to support you, meaning I want to motivate you, empower you, and hopefully inspire you to continue with your journey. The first thing I need you to know is that I genuinely care about you becoming a better leader because I know exactly what you're going through. And to prove it, I'm going to put my money where my mouth is. I'm going to open up for a moment and reveal to you that I'm a regular, flawed, awkward, and genuine human being. The same as everyone else.

\*\*\*

When I think about the fact that my dog Polly (the seven-year-old boxer mix snoring in the living room right now, classic Polly) will eventually pass away, I usually work myself up into tears. I could be having the best day ever, and if I start to dwell on the fact that I only have a finite amount of time left with her, I turn into a sentimental mess. I don't need to explain the bond people have with their pets, and I will be an absolute wreck when she is no longer with our family (I will sob for days).

I grew a mustache because I think it balances my face out. I have a ginormous nose, which I was constantly made fun of for as a kid ("Hey Big Bird"), and I think the new soup strainer helps even all of "this" out. *(Gestures to face.)* The fact that I now resemble a GI Joe from the 1980s is just a perk,

I suppose. And worth noting while on the subject—I was incessantly bullied as a kid for a multitude of other reasons (and I remember it all), a fact that I have only ever shared with a few people.

My favorite show in high school was the teen drama (soap) *The O.C.* It's the only full-series DVD set that I still own today. I don't even have a DVD player anymore, so I'm not sure what's going on there. Oh, and I used to wear puka shell necklaces too. Horrific, I know.

We all have that one artist, band, or musician that is our guilty pleasure. Mine is Adele. When I was in grad school, I was obsessed with her song "Hello" and probably listened to it (and sang it out loud) forty thousand times.

One of my favorite breakfasts is mashing up an avocado and then mixing in uncooked old-fashioned oats. I don't know why, but the texture and flavor can't be beat. Most people think I'm nuts for doing this, and I really can't argue with their logic.

I keep Listerine strips and mouthwash within reach at all times (in the car, in my backpack, at work). My wife tells me I have a problem (and so does my dentist). If I think my breath is even an 8.5 out of 10, I take action. Around other people or just alone in the house, I can't stand bad breath, and the thought of having it kicks my compulsive brain into overdrive.

In college, I was a Segway tour guide in Duluth, Minnesota. A team of us would teach people how to ride them, and then I would take the group on a guided tour of the Lake Superior Bay area. My Segway skills are still next level.

And here's one that should give you nightmares and permanently haunt your dreams: Joe Reichert in the third grade.

I am as normal as it gets. I don't pretend to be a stoic leadership guru with all the answers. Just someone with a passion for leading and teaching others.

*∗*

For better or worse, I'm a realist. I came to the conclusion that I was never going to be a professional athlete long before my wonderful, caring, and supportive mother ever did. There's nothing wrong with setting lofty goals, but I also think it's important to set ones that are achievable.

We both want you to go on and become an amazing leader and change the lives of everyone you come in contact with from now until—forever. To one day motivate, inspire, and empower thousands of people in whatever path life takes you. However, my goal for us during our time together is a bit more measured.

All I want—true success in my mind—is for you to leave here feeling a bit more prepared to become a leader. To think to yourself, *It's not that scary, I can do that*, and feel ready to take your next steps into leadership. That's it. And here's my deviously straightforward plan: show you what leadership actually is, then describe in detail how to actually become one. The essentials—no more, no less.

# Chapter 5
## The Tiny Fire

Nothing bummed me out more as a ten-year-old than watching the magical permed afro of Bob Ross put a giant tree smack dab in the middle of what was otherwise a masterpiece. Every Saturday morning, I'd wake up to watch him dazzle us with mountains, streams, and endless hills of colorful bushes. You can probably hear his smooth-jazz voice in your head right now. Each week, he taught countless men, women, and children how to paint, how to make our very own "happy little accidents." Bob (the expert) painted; we watched, then did our absolute best to emulate it at the kitchen table. But in those eleven years on public television, do you know the phrase that was never once uttered by Mr. Ross during one of his tapings? "Everyone, I'm so sorry to ask this, but could you just look away for a moment? I'm not feeling too confident about this one. It's not quite ready yet."

Of course not, because that would've been ridiculous. The whole point of the show was to learn from an expert and watch him at his craft. Bob, our teacher—confident in his skills—let us in to see how the sausage was made. There wasn't a doubt in his mind that eventually, some twenty-eight minutes later, a masterpiece would ensue. That right there is the difference confidence can make, and it's the reason that when I would draw something in school, the exact opposite would happen.

I would feverishly hide my artwork from anyone trying to get a glimpse before it was "ready." It's also the reason I won't let my wife peek over my shoulder and read what I've written here until after it's been polished up. And it's the same reason so many people wanting to go into leadership keep it a secret from the rest of the world.

Picture your leadership skills today as a small flame inside of you, deep in your rib cage. One day, it will be a roaring wildfire, able to withstand the elements and grow to be a self-sustaining fireball. You'll proudly open up and shine your light for others to see, fully embracing the role of a superb leader. However, at this point, the best way to describe your flame is as a tiny secret. In fact, I would bet you acquired this book without confiding in a single soul that you want to become a leader. It really is a *secret* flame that you're guarding. "Everyone look away, it's not ready yet."

And I totally get it. You don't want to embarrass yourself by telling someone who, regrettably, isn't supportive thereby getting even one piece of negative feedback. It's just too risky. So, you do what most of us do—hide it. Protect the flame at all costs. Shield your desire for a career in leadership from any negative weather (other people) that might be passing by. Because you find yourself thinking—*What if I fail? What if this is stupid and a complete waste of time? What if Mom was right and I should've hopelessly kept trying to play in the NBA?*

Now, if you do this for too long, your flame, like all tiny fires, will be smothered—and in the process, you will extinguish your goal of one day becoming an extraordinary leader. But I'm here to tell you that it's perfectly normal to be hiding your tiny leadership flame at this moment. Some people would advise you, "Shout your goals from the rooftops and make it known you want to be a leader. Grab life by the beanbag and turn your dream into a reality this instant!" and the truth of it is, those people telling you that—are idiots.

The first "leadership thing" I am going to share with you is that everybody is different. What works for X's personality type might actually be cruel and unusual punishment for Y's. It could result in X achieving their goals and Y being put off for a lifetime. This book is not "Do this exact thing and become a leader." That book belongs in the trash. There are billions of paths to becoming an effective and life-changing leader. If you know the absolute basics of leadership—the stuff I'm about to teach you—then you don't need to worry about fitting into a mold or, as we saw from my mistake while coaching, attempting to be someone you're not.

I want to reassure you: at the end of this book, you will still be you—with all the beautiful flaws and quirky goodness that only you possess. Except now you'll be primed and ready to go out into the world with a self-sustaining leadership fireball. Which is why, right now, I have only one goal for myself over the next two chapters: keep your tiny flame alive. When you're a bit more ready, we are going to give it some air (and gasoline). However, in this moment, reading this sentence—your secret is safe with me.

✻✻✻

As often as I reference your leadership flame, there is, unfortunately, one thing I can't help you with—the spark. The step before the tiny flame where you decided "I want to be a leader." That can only come from you, and it's the single prerequisite for reading this book (it's either in there or it's not). Leaders are important. They're crucial, in fact. They take their teams to levels of success most never thought possible, and the great ones will forever change the lives of almost everyone they come in contact with. But you don't need piles of data to tell you that. Which means I won't attempt to convince anyone to become a leader in this book.

Transforming into a leader isn't something a person can be coerced or paid to do. And it's the reason you won't find data or research in here on why leaders are important, or why the people around you need you to be an amazing leader for them, or why, in my opinion, it's the best decision you'll make in your entire life. All I can do is guide you on how to become one—I can't determine whether that's somewhere you want to go.

What you'll find is that a lot of leadership resources are (oddly) statistical in nature. They bombard you with polls, research, and surveys to prove to you that it's worthwhile to become a leader. "Do X as a leader and you'll achieve Y; leaders with this trait end up being XX percent more productive than those without it; teams with great leaders are X times more successful than ones without." But they lack a very simple and often overlooked component of leadership—the human element. Leaders are humans. The people we lead, also humans. And that's what we're after: becoming a real-life leader to other real-life people.

# Chapter 6
## Guarding the Flame

If someone sends you a fire emoji, one of two things is happening: they either find you *muy caliente*, or you're in imminent danger. I doubt that whoever discovered fire, with their Stone Age social skills and lack of evolutionary foresight, could've ever dreamed it would one day be compared to and used for so many things. You can cook with it, see with it, warm up with it, roast marshmallows with it, and send it through the phone. And yet, for how amazingly useful fires are, my fu*king word, it's hard to start a fire when you really need one.

Once they get going, and under the right conditions, you're golden. Until that point—look out. Cue you and your leadership flame. Given the fragile state it's in right now, we need to go over the most common ways I've seen other people's flames get extinguished. Unfortunately, like in *March of the Penguins,* not everyone that sets out on this journey makes it to the end. Some will fail very early on, and for others, it could happen days or even years from now. I've seen it all, and I want to prepare you as best I can to guarantee this doesn't happen to you.

\*\*\*

The *immediate fail* is probably the toughest one for me to swallow. The biggest reason this happens, and one that is no longer an issue for you since you're reading this book, is that people simply don't know where to start. They get overwhelmed. They search "Leadership Book" on Amazon and get 4 billion results, or they wake up to find themselves down a YouTube rabbit hole, having scrolled through hours of mind-numbing content. Water is a great flavorless beverage that we need to survive, but it can actually kill you in two ways: dehydration and water poisoning. Consuming gallons of it at a time can be just as deadly as not drinking enough. The former is where many find themselves when first starting out. I wasn't joking earlier—the stage you're currently at can be unbelievably confusing, leading to an anxiety-ridden process of finding a good place to simply *start*. Which can, unfortunately, trigger the dangerous thought of "I'll get to it, but just not today."

Now I doubt it gives anyone tangible anxiety, but deciphering a good starting place will seem like more work than it's worth—meaning it will never take precedence in your busy life. So, there it sits at the bottom, with learning French and buying a Peloton, never to resurface again.

The other type of immediate fail happens when a person's first leadership resource doesn't resonate with them, thus extinguishing their flame. For whatever reason, the first book they read, TED Talk they watch, or course they enroll in just doesn't hit the mark. Maybe it wasn't all that good. Or maybe it was great but for whatever reason didn't click for them. Either way, this unfortunate scenario can turn someone off from the subject forever. Bad YouTube videos are nothing new, but when it's your first step into leadership, it really stinks. When this happens, leadership is now associated with—whatever that was—for eternity.

The final reason for an immediate fail is that a person's first experience as a new leader goes poorly. Maybe they mistakenly open up and show their tiny leadership flame to someone who isn't supportive, or they try to step up and lead a project for the first time and it doesn't go well. In either case, the thought of being a leader has left a permanent bad taste in their mouth.

"Maybe they're right, I wouldn't be a good leader because of . . ."

"Well, that went poorly, never doing that again."

"But Michael Scott makes it seem so easy . . ."

Note: If this has happened to you, I admire your perseverance for sticking it out and giving leadership another shot. I've certainly had my share of bad managers (the kind that make your skin crawl), and I have been told countless times that I wasn't the right fit to be a leader because of my personality. Fu*k them, and fu*k that. Anyone can be a great leader. Including you and me.

***

The next type of leadership fail I see is the *slightly-longer-than-immediate fail*. It's the most common type to find at the office because it has everything to do with intent. Not quite an immediate fail because the individual leaves the launchpad, but they've got a fatal flaw—they're not doing it for the right reasons. Internal fires are just that—internal. My own leadership flame cannot sustain someone else's. I could use a flamethrower and send you mine all day long, but it would only be surface deep, and as soon as I removed it, yours too would fade away. At the end of the day, the motivation to become a leader must be your own. As clichéd as it sounds—you really do have to want to be here.

This is why most corporate leadership programs have such poor long-term results. (They'll never tell employees this, but I've seen the special sauce.) There's an ass-backwards idea that we can somehow pay people to become leaders. I've been in actual meetings where HR has told me, "We can't expect someone to do this on their own time, away from work. We have to find a way to compensate them for learning about leadership, or they'll never do it." Quite possibly one of the saddest statements I've ever heard, and an ominous sign for any organization that feels this way. Not trying to be a wet towel, but nobody can pay you to do this. It simply won't work.

Although it's a tempting comparison, leadership is not at all like running a marathon. You can train and run a race to impress someone, or on another's behalf. There is a designated finish line. Even if you're going through hell, it's finite, making it not quite so terrible. "I can get through this. I can endure." Leadership, on the other hand, is a lifelong pursuit. Becoming one, and more importantly, staying one, will define you for the remainder of your days on earth. Being something you're not passionate about, something you don't really want to be, for a lifetime isn't feasible. Nobody can make you become a leader. And you can't become a leader for someone else. That's not how it works.

Now, I'm not here to tell you what the right reasons are for embarking on this journey—those are solely for you to decide—but I do know wrong reasons when I see them. Here are a couple:

I like being the boss and in charge.

I want to make more money.

Do you think Nelson Mandela woke up one day and said to himself, "You know what, I like telling people what to do. I should become president"? No, he did not. Did Mother Teresa confide in a friend, "I'm really just doing all of this so I can get paid and buy a Ferrari"? Hell-on-earth no. Every great leader has had their own unique motivators—their right reasons—and I'm certain being in charge or making more money wasn't on the list.

\*\*\*

The last set of leadership-flame extinguishers to watch out for fall into the *failing later* category. As a society, we have this misconceived notion that doing something for a long time makes you an expert at it. You've probably heard of Malcolm Gladwell's 10,000-Hour Rule—that it takes ten thousand hours of intensive practice to become a master in something. A direct correlation between time spent and mastery of a skill. Yoda (the green fictional Star Wars character) is a great example of this theory. The older Yoda gets, the wiser he becomes. As it relates to leadership mastery, we incorrectly default to the same logic.

Mistakenly, we assume that managers and executives who have performed these duties for a long time are somehow better leaders because of it. That their long history of being in charge has somehow allowed them to reach leadership nirvana, rendering them excellent leaders. So then riddle me this: Why have I had horrible bosses (whether it be degrading, inappropriate, or just purely lacking in engagement) that have been doing their job for longer than I've been alive?

The reason is that leadership is different. It's not the piano, and as such, it can't be treated the same way a simple skill can. When you play the wrong note as a piano student, you hear it immediately. It's obvious to anyone in the room that—whoops—clearly a mistake has been made. So, you go back and correct yourself—"Don't hit that key again"—and away you go. Eventually, the errors are fewer and farther between as you learn the dos and don'ts of reading music. Most jobs and functional duties are like this. Study a subject for long enough, and you will inevitably know more about it than a newcomer would. Years and years of experience that have built upon one another usually make someone a master in their subject matter. Developing as a leader is not even remotely the same.

Being a leader means dealing with other people. Unfortunately, there is no buzzer that goes off when actions are taken that don't embody a good leader. When a manager interacts with someone and it isn't up to code for being a "Leadership Yoda" (whether they know it or not) there's no awkward sound to inform the boss that they need to be better in the future.

This is failing later. An individual is up and running as someone with functional authority (a coach, a manager, a vice president)—but to the detriment of themselves and everyone they're in charge of leading, they're practicing the wrong things. A poor foundation of bad habits is keeping them in the "terrible boss" rut for eternity—destined to forever ruin the lives of those around them. The ways to avoid this are actually pretty simple: have a solid understanding of what leadership actually is, and be strong enough to critique yourself as a leader while you progress in your career. It is a personal journey, and the only way to become a great leader is by continually holding yourself accountable.

Leadership is something truly remarkable. It gets compared to a lot of things, but ultimately there's nothing quite like it. No shortcuts or cheat codes to send you directly to the finish line. No set of rules or instruction manuals that will realign you when things go off the rails. Just a personal endeavor filled with ups and downs and lessons to be learned along the way. Nobody expects you to put this book down and instantly become an exceptional, world-altering leader. No. But I do ask that you care enough to stay the course when things get difficult, and to always remember why you're here. To always come back to your leadership flame, and to eventually help others in growing their own.

# Chapter 7
## What to Expect

Plop. Into the water.

Out of the water.

Into the water. Out of the water.

Imagine for a moment that you've spent your entire life to this point as a little green turtle. Round with stubby legs and a shell too big for your body, you spend most of your days hanging out at quiet ponds, sunbathing for hours while you ponder the meaning of life. And, like clockwork, at the end of every day, you curl up on a warm rock with good friends to discuss current events. Life is good. It's consistent, predictable, and rarely full of surprises.

Then one day while taking a nap on the shore, you wake up to a strange tingly sensation. Inside your miniature body, things start to feel off—like you've had a caffeine injection to your turtle jugular. An avid comic book fan, you recognize what's going on: somehow, you've started to acquire supernatural powers. Perhaps it was a fly you ate, or that giant gulp of lake water after lunch, but you are certain that Marvel superpowers are on their way to you. As you go to bed that night, you hope for a mix of Thor and Wolverine, just please not Ant-Man.

The next morning, you slowly peel your eyes open and are shocked at what you find in the mirror—giant pelican wings now protruding from your shell. Feathery, majestic appendages that were clearly not there when you went to bed. That morning is a mess—figuring out how to make toast, how to lie on your side, how to go to the bathroom—it's slow going, but eventually you start finding your way. And after days of trial and error, you awkwardly figure out how to flap your wings, and one day you even begin to fly.

Through practice, crashes, and emergency landings, you start getting pretty good. Soon you're flying all over town, "Look Mom, there's Pico, the turtle bird." You're seeing and experiencing things you never could've dreamed of. You help other animals across the intersection, deliver milk to the turtle elderly, and can finally flip yourself over like a pancake.

Now, imagine you go back to your local pond to see some friends. It's a small watering hole and always packed to the gills, so you fold your wings up under your shell for the night. And even though your wings aren't out in plain sight, you still feel different. You have an air about you. A confidence. An invisible yet easily noticeable self-purpose. Turtles you've known for years look at you and say, "Pico, you seem different." And likewise, everyone else seems different to you now that you've seen the world as a turtle bird. You're no longer landlocked Pico; you can fly. You've experienced one of the greatest wonders the world has to offer, flight, and you're using it to make a difference for those around you. That night your turtle friends can't see your wings, but they all recognize that you're not the same Pico they grew up with. And that's because you aren't. Which is exactly what becoming a leader is like: a turtle that sprouts wings. It's certainly not a bad thing, but it's worth noting so you can be prepared for it when it happens to you.

***

Your whole life is about to change. For the better, of course, but things are going to be different. Once you become a leader, how you view and interact with the world will never be the same. Likewise, how people view and interact with you will be fundamentally altered as well. Below is a list of situations. I'd like you to determine how you would act or respond today in each of them.

You see someone at work spill coffee on their shirt.

You're in a rush and the server has made a mistake on your bill.

You forget to ring up an item from your grocery cart.

These situations are nothing outrageous. In fact, they appear to be pretty benign daily interactions, which is why I think they are such a good test of character. Most of us would already answer the examples below with what a good leader (or just human being) would do:

A friend of yours is relapsing back into an addictive behavior.

You realize a team member is going through a difficult period at home.

You see someone embezzling funds and hear they are starting a fight club.

Scenarios like these aren't all that useful because they're so drastic. It's blatantly obvious (or at least quasi-obvious) what the "correct" answers are. It doesn't take an expert-level leader to figure them out.

Here's the real test, though. I want you to reexamine the first list of encounters, except this time with the caveat that in every one of them, you are having a horrible day. Bloody nose, completely out of coffee, stubbed two toes and the car won't start type of morning. Pick your poison, but it just isn't going your way. How do you answer them now? Does anything change? Do your own inconveniences impact how you interact with the world? They might today, but I think you'll be surprised when you come back in five years and re-answer them. Then have another look in fifteen years. To the time-traveling leader version of yourself—*I wasn't kidding, was I?*

And these scenarios aren't some magical checklist I've come up with to help determine leaders versus nonleaders; they're just simple examples of how everyday life changes when you become one. As you rewire your brain, you'll no longer be the old you. You'll still be amazing, brilliant, and probably all-around awesome, except now it will be as the leader version of yourself. You'll look the same. You'll probably even smell the same. Except now, everywhere you go and every aspect of life you encounter, you will do so with your leadership wings. Every relationship you have—friends, teammates, coworkers, loved ones—will change. How you view and interact with them, and how they view and interact with you, will be different. And try as you might, these wings will be seared onto you as long as you remain a practicing leader.

It's not going to be easy (we'll get to that), and there will be days you want to throw in the towel (completely normal, by the way), but becoming an amazing leader is something that every person on earth can achieve.

# Chapter 8
## There Are No "Leaders"

Back when I was an ugly child, my mother used to tell me that I'd forget my head if it wasn't attached to my shoulders. And she's not lying. I've had a terrible memory for as long as I can remember. I forget birthdays, grocery items, and especially names. I've known a guy at my gym for 3 years. I haven't used his name since I forgot it 2.5 years ago, and we say hello to each other every day. "Hey, Joe." "Hey ... *Buddy*." At this point, it's just too embarrassing to ask, and it's the same way at work. Though thankfully, with our shift to a hybrid work environment, when I'm in a meeting with someone online, their name is up in front of me the entire time, all but making it impossible for me to repeat my gym guy ordeal with anyone else.

The other piece of information I inevitably know about someone in an online meeting is their job title. Winston Schmidt, marketing associate. Leslie Knope, deputy director. David Rose, manager. If you can dream it, you can probably find someone, somewhere, with that title. There is, however, one title I have yet to ever come across at work, one I've never seen posted on a job site, and one I've never had anyone use to introduce themselves.

I'd like you to take a moment and think of the three best leaders you've had in your life (and if that's a stretch, you can use famous leaders you know of). Three people who really stick out to you. People you absolutely consider to be good leaders. Now, next to their names, I want you to put what their official titles were. Maybe they were a head coach, a manager, a vice president, a teacher, a nurse, or an engineer. There are over a billion job titles out there, and often people have more than one, but I want you to identify what titles your leaders had.

Now, whenever I speak to groups of new leaders, I always do this same exercise, and in all my times doing it, there is only one title I've never heard someone say: leader.

Strange, right?

Take out your phone and try to find a job posting for just a *leader* online. You're probably able to find *leader of (blank)* or *(blank) team lead*, but just that singular word *leader* as a title—the word you thought of when making your mental list—doesn't exist. Yet you know these people were leaders, so clearly being a leader must be something different. And if at this point you've started thinking *WTF is going on?* then you're exactly right—WTF indeed. We are completely detaching ourselves from the old notion of what a leader is, the one we've been force-fed for decades now, and this process of altering our minds can be painful at first.

***

The year was 1997; Leonardo DiCaprio was sent sinking to the bottom of the Atlantic in *Titanic*, the domain name "google.com" was first registered, and Steve Jobs was named the interim CEO of Apple. A lesser-known fact—it was also the year that future Hollywood front man Chris Pratt graduated from high school and was voted the class clown by his peers. If you've seen Pratt in one of his many hit roles (*Parks & Rec, Guardians of the Galaxy, Jurassic World*), this shouldn't come as a surprise to you. His command of the screen and ability to inject any situation with a jolt of humor was recognized early on by his classmates at Lake Stevens High

School. Pratt, whose official title at school was *student*, conducted himself in a manner that others found humorous. Being silly, cracking jokes, and making people laugh earned him the role of the class clown.

Titles are directly tied to the functional duties you perform on the team. Roles are something completely different. For Chris, it looked like the following:

- Functional Duty = Student
  ◇ Attend class, complete assigned work, pass exams, and graduate
- Role = Class Clown
  ◇ Act in a silly and fun-loving manner while a student

During his time at Lake Stevens, Chris was always a student, and regardless of whether he was funny, he would have remained a student. However, the way he behaved on a daily basis earned him a role on the team (the Lake Stevens student body). This distinction was not something he applied for, and it did not change the fact that, as a student, he was still required to fulfill the functional duties associated with being one. Instead, the class clown role was given to him as a result of how he handled himself while satisfying those responsibilities. This is the difference between functions and roles—an often misunderstood delineation, and the key to understanding how regular people can become extraordinary leaders.

Official titles can be found hovering above your name in an online meeting or nestled up under your picture on LinkedIn. "Joe Reichert, Manager." They identify to the world what your function is on your current team. Or, more specifically to work, what your job duties are.

- Manager: set team deliverables and define employee tasking
- Teacher: prepare and deliver lesson plans to students
- Vice President: define and implement corporate strategy

- Head Coach: prepare the team and execute the game plan

But the roles on a team are something completely different. These are how people see you. They're things you become; you can earn them. How you conduct yourself while satisfying your functional duties determines the way others view you and thus the role they give to you. It's why no one on your list had the formal title of leader. If you look back, you'll notice how I worded the question: people you *consider* to be leaders. I didn't ask you to think of three people whose title was specifically *leader*. Being a leader is a role that must be *earned*, exactly like those leaders did with you.

Now, does everyone on your list have the exact same title, or can different functions occupy the leader role? Do this exercise with one hundred different people, and you uncover something special—there's actually no correlation between a person's function and their ability to be considered a leader. The responses run the gamut, proving there is no requirement for which functions can become a leader (they are completely independent from one another)— and solidifying the often quoted saying that "Anyone can become a leader." Any person, in any function, can be a leader in the eyes of someone else.

Finally, examine your list of leaders for anyone that didn't have a title. Did anyone have absolutely no functional duties on their team? No, because what would that even look like? What would "Taylor Thompson, Leader" even do at work? To obtain the leader role, you must be a part of the team and have your own functional duty—it just doesn't matter which one.

***

I don't blame anyone for finding this confusing. For decades, we've been combining functions and roles and referring to them interchangeably, creating synonyms in the process that often do more harm than good. The biggest culprit is the constant exchange of *leader* with *manager*, which has resulted in the greatest myth of our time—that being a manager automatically makes someone a leader. If you've ever had a bad boss, the type that couldn't care less about you as a human being, then you know this isn't true.

Sadly, we've all been a part of teams where the manager (or person in charge) was not a great leader. Just a dirtbag concerned with only one thing: themselves. Those teams did have people on them that I considered to be leaders; it just wasn't the boss.

In fact, on multiple occasions in my life, the leader role has been occupied by someone with functional duties not traditionally associated with leadership: data architect, modeling and simulation engineer, backup running back. Folks who embodied what a leader should be and would make my own top ten list, but who lacked a job title that is normally considered synonymous with a leader.

The inverse of this is also true: it's possible to be a great manager and a poor leader. Setting deliverables, defining your team's vision, and delegating tasks are all standard duties for a manager. But unfortunately, you can treat people like garbage and still achieve all of those. As I've warned many young leaders at work who aspire to be managers—you can be a pretty terrible person to your employees and still receive high marks for your impact on the business. Your team may crumble from attrition, and HR may eventually pay you a visit, but there is usually nothing in a manager's job description that dictates *how* those tasks are achieved, only that they are completed. Those horrible bosses still wake up the next day with their title of *manager*.

Here is a real job posting I found online for a manager. Please tell me where in this list of responsibilities it's dictated how they are accomplished.

- ensures project results and customer deliverables meet requirements regarding technical quality, reliability, schedule, and cost
- participates in budget development and evaluating how project plan changes impact cost and schedule

- works collaboratively with the program director on managing vacancies, onboarding, work allocation, and associated activities to ensure program staffing meets customer requirements
- participates in the proposal process and supports the generation of new business

My point exactly. And I can tell you that as a manager at a Fortune 500 company, at the end of the year, I am only graded on whether I meet those obligations. Zero percent of my potential salary increase is impacted by whether I treated people well or acted like a leader should. It's assumed that effective leadership is happening, when in reality, we all know this isn't always the case. Yet this separation of leadership and management eludes most people and companies today. I've brought up this issue at work, and people look at me like I just ordered nuggets off the children's menu.

✻✻✻

"For the record, you're not going to like this" is how I start every conversation when someone asks me to speak in front of one of our leadership development programs at work. And it doesn't take long for them to realize I'm not kidding. "Hello everyone, before I begin today, I'd like you all to answer this question openly and honestly in your heads. Are you a better leader today—right now at this very moment—than when you started the program?" Dazed faces stare back at me. "Not, 'Are you better at finance or engineering or computing earned value metrics?' Are you a better *leader*?" At which point, I set the tone for the next twenty minutes: "If the answer is no, then it's safe to say that you are wasting your time." It's an effective talk, but no, I rarely get asked back.

Companies all around the world waste exorbitant amounts of money every year trying in vain to develop leaders due to an inability to differentiate management from leadership. They focus on the wrong things in their curriculum, then get frustrated when they churn out managers that can't lead their way out of a paper bag. They fund misguided trainings, seminars, and networking events that have literally nothing to do with learning about actual leadership. Now, I'm not against participating in these programs to advance one's career, but if the goal is to produce managers, call it what it is—management development—because it certainly isn't leadership development.

Even the universities we're all indebted to struggle with this. A few years ago, I completed a master's degree in organizational leadership, and as I look back on it, it didn't do diddly for me as a leader. Below are the courses I completed, which were intended to one day (allegedly) prepare me to earn the leader role.

| | |
|---|---|
| Yes (but misguided) | Effective Organizations: Theory and Practice |
| Yes (but misguided) | Dynamics of Power in Organizations |
| Nope | Business Ethics and Corporate Social Responsibility |
| Nope | Decision Theory in a Global Marketplace |
| Nope | Contemporary Business Writing and Communication |
| Yes! | Leading Diverse Teams |
| Nope | Technology Management in the Global Economy |
| Nope | Strategic Product Innovation |
| Yes (but misguided) | Examination of Modern Leadership |
| Nope | Qualitative and Quantitative Research Methods |

It's worth reiterating: these courses were for a degree in leadership. Not management. Not business. Organizational leadership—leading other humans at a place of business. If you are thinking about doing one of these degrees, yes, it will pad the résumé and help you get a job in management. No, it will probably not teach you anything remotely useful about how to actually be a leader.

This is the radioactive and forever hazardous fallout from using *manager* and *leader* as synonyms: a perpetual misconception that the specific functions of a manager, director, VP, or CEO are, at their core, what makes someone a leader. Logic would then tell us that in order to make more leaders, we need to teach more people how to perform those functions better, which ultimately begs the question (and one I hear constantly from aspiring leaders): "So if I don't have the opportunity to do one of those duties as part of my job, can I even be a leader?" Yes, you can. One thousand times yes. Functional duties have nothing to do with the role you earn on the team.

✳✳✳

At Lake Stevens High School, it was common knowledge that Chris Pratt was funny. As a freshman and up to the start of his senior year, everyone knew: that guy is hilarious. However, if, in some strange turn of events, Pratt entered his senior year intending to no longer be his lighthearted self, and he adopted a much more serious and stoic manner—well then, his classmates would've thought to themselves, "That's odd. Chris seems different. He's changed." He still would have been a student, but he would no longer be known as the funny guy on campus, and he wouldn't have been voted the class clown by his peers at the end of the year. That's the thing about roles—they're really only lent to you.

Functional duties (titles) are static, and like late-night tattoos, they're not coming off. If you want to change your function, you have to apply to a new one. For better or worse, for the time being, they're all yours. But the roles on a team are something completely different. These are things you earn from other people. But if the people on your team no longer see you in that way, then you no longer occupy that role. Which is why, wishful thinkers and students of leadership, I love you—but you're not leaders. You have to go out and actively earn the leader role from the people around you all the time. How people view you, and thus the role you earn, is related to how you fulfill your duties. Change your behavior, and it will, in turn, change how they perceive you. And it's like this at work, at home, and on every other team you're a part of.

# Chapter 9
## A World of Teams

Without question, he's the greatest to ever play the game. Not only did he win six NBA championships (twice going back-to-back-to-back), but he also saved the planet from a Looney-Tunes apocalypse with Bill Murray in the movie *Space Jam*. So, in a weird way, we owe Michael Jordan a lot more than just respect for his skills on the basketball court. In fact, he was so good that we use his name as a benchmark for greatness: "Nick is like the Michael Jordan of eating hot dogs. That guy's a machine." The shoes, the clothes, the crying memes—MJ continues to be everywhere. The greatest player, who played on some of the greatest teams the world has ever seen. One of which was the 1995–96 Chicago Bulls.

Michael Jordan, Scottie Pippen, the "Worm" Dennis Rodman—amazing players utilized to perfection by head coach Phil Jackson. That year, the Bulls won a record seventy-two games in the regular season, and went on to handily take home the NBA championship. This never-before-seen success can be attributed to only one thing: an amazing team. Yes, having the best player to ever grace the game in "His Airness" Michael Jordan certainly helps, but in the years that MJ played without Pippen, Rodman, and Jackson, he won exactly zero NBA championships.

It's a team sport. Thirteen players, a head coach, assistant coaches, the front office, talent scouts, the person selling you your tickets on game day—all part of one giant team. People with vastly different functional duties (point guard, accountant, groundskeeper), all working together toward a shared goal: making the Bulls the best team in the National Basketball Association. There were leaders sprinkled throughout the organization, but on the court and for the players, none were more influential than head coach Phil Jackson.

Jackson was great at his function as a basketball coach. His offensive scheme and the way he leveraged his players' skill sets in perfect harmony are major reasons why the Chicago Bulls were so successful in the '90s. Yet it was his ability to understand his players, and build meaningful connections with them, that enabled him to motivate and empower his team to their full potential (both as players and people). He did what was right for his team all the time, serving as the head coach and team leader. I'd suggest watching the Netflix docuseries *The Last Dance* to see this in action. Although the series covers a different season than the one I'm referencing, you can still get an idea for how Phil Jackson led that team to amazing success. Truly an incredible team.

Conversely, one of the worst teams in recent history has been the ride-hailing company Uber. Marred by tragedy, mismanagement, and a systemic culture of sexual harassment in the workplace, Uber has been nothing short of inept since its founding in 2009 by former CEO Travis Kalanick. Although widely popular, this organization has done its absolute best to slow progress at every turn. Whether in the form of Kalanick being caught on camera swearing at an Uber driver, the company's questionable business practices, or blog posts bringing to light sexual harassment within the company, horrible leadership has been the calling card of Uber. The goal of Uber (like any for-profit corporation) is to generate revenue via selling a product or service. Everyone employed on the Uber team, regardless of where they land within the organization, ultimately shares this goal. Different functional duties all working together toward a shared goal—that's the definition of a team (except in this case, a terrible one).

Another example of a team, and one that annoys the living sh*t out of me, is my homeowners' association. The processes involved with making changes to our house have me, at times, pining for a hermit's life up in the mountains. But despite my frustrations, I appreciate what they do, and I know they mean well—they're simply trying to ensure safety and aesthetic standards for the neighborhood (the HOA's overarching goal). Front office workers, design review board members, and community managers—all different functional duties working together to make our neighborhood better.

Teams are easy to spot when they're this formal and clearly defined. They have names with logos, we get paychecks from them, you can use profanities to describe your displeasure with them. However, in our day-to-day lives, they're a bit trickier to spot. (Most don't wear jerseys.)

Take my gym, for example. Every morning at 5:30 a.m., I lug my rapidly deteriorating body down the road to get a workout in. I'm not employed there, so it's not the company that is my team. Rather, I'm a gym-goer and on a team with my fellow gym-goers. At first you may think we are a random assortment of people with nothing linking us together, when, in actuality, we all have a shared goal: getting in better shape. And though some of us may never speak to one another, we all share this bond. Our functional duties are as members of the gym—and within that team, roles can, and do, emerge.

We could do this forever, listing teams, but I think you get the picture—our world is broken up into teams. Millions upon millions of teams, comprised of people that each have their own overlapping network of teams. It sounds like a lot, but we're all surprisingly versed in this seemingly chaotic landscape.

\*\*\*

If I told you I'm visiting family over the holidays, you'd have a pretty good idea of who I'll be spending time with. But you couldn't be certain because I, like everyone, have multiple uses of the word *family*. There is the nuclear family I grew up with and am still a part of (parents, brother, sisters), my extended family (aunts, uncles, cousins, grandparents, nieces, nephews), my newest nuclear family since I got married (wife, dog), the family I married into (my wife's original nuclear family), her extended family, and finally, the entire collection of people I just named as my larger *family*. And in each instance, my function is slightly different (my family "job title," so to speak). To my parents I'm a son, to my wife I'm a husband, and to my nieces and nephews I'm the uncle that sneaks them fireworks and sour candy. I'm all these things, all the time, but it's easy to keep it straight since I'm usually not acting as all of them simultaneously (we would need a stadium-sized venue for that gathering). The family "hat" we're wearing depends on who we are around. Each one of them a team of connected individuals (this time a result of being related) working together toward a shared goal—in this case, of preserving and facilitating the needs of those in the family.

Other examples of teams I am a part of include the company I work for, the small engineering team I manage at that company, the leadership development program I started, the crew I golf with on Friday mornings, my Denver suburb community, the Saturday-morning dog park posse, and so on. Regardless of how large they are—two people or two hundred thousand—they're all teams, each with its own shared goal. A common, often unacknowledged (and rarely written down) purpose that on some level binds those people together. Winning or generating revenue usually comes to mind first, but survival, success, and general enjoyment are three other common shared goals we encounter within our teams on a daily basis.

"But Joe, sometimes I'm around a random assortment of people—how can that be a team?"

\*\*\*

Remember those little white floaty things you'd pluck off dandelions and blow into the wind as a kid? They're called pappi, and on gusty days, they scatter into the air and become enemy number one for our dog Polly, who chomps at them as they blow by (bless her heart, she's never got one). With no rhyme or reason as to where they end up, and no binding force to keep them tethered to one another, they truly are at the whim of the wind. Randomly scattered in all directions like molecules in space, a group of pappi in motion. And the one thing you'll never see is an orb of pappi moving around in unison—a fluffy white sphere maintaining a cohesive shape, paranormally floating together across the field from place to place. Because that would be terrifying—and simply unrealistic behavior for them.

Without some sort of binding force, objects in our universe will scatter aimlessly, which is why it's exceedingly rare to spot a truly random group of people on our planet. In fact, they're almost nonexistent. It's a bit counterinitiative because our instinct is to think, "If I don't know these people, how can we possibly be associated with one another, let alone be on a team together?" Well, for starters, if any of us are in the same location and doing the same activity, this rules out being part of a random group. Like molecules in the atmosphere or pappi in the wind, humans don't just collect for no reason. This is what makes *groups* of people almost impossible to find. True randomness, at its core, means there is nothing associating one object to another, nothing keeping them together. So just like particles, a random assortment of people, when brought together, will immediately disburse.

The grocery store is a great example of this. Although you do not know most people there, you are all bound together in a single location by your desire to purchase food. For the duration you are there, you are a part of that team. The same holds for when you're at a concert. You don't know everyone in the crowd, but you are all choosing to be colocated (the exact opposite of random scattering) in order to hear and enjoy the music. When someone near you has had five too many White Claws and is ruining the show, everyone impacted gets upset. This inebriated mess is putting the team's goal in danger—a goal you all share.

For the duration of that Lady Gaga concert, you are all part of that team. If you went there with a collection of friends, you were a part of two teams while there. If you ran into a group of coworkers, that makes three teams. Perhaps you were all citizens of the same country—four teams, and so on. Most of those will exist after the show ends (you're not in that team's company anymore, though you're still a member), but sometimes teams, like musical performances, come and go. If you were to write down all the teams you are a part of on a daily basis, it might freak you out. An overwhelming number, every day, overlapping one another. And unless you live in the wilderness, completely remote, with no family and zero contact with the outside world, then you are without a doubt on at least a few teams. No matter how hard some may try, there are no lone wolves anymore, only teams. And it's within these teams that the leader role emerges.

✳✳✳

I have an impossible task for you—find someone at work who does not have a title. No job duty, no functions to perform, no reason for being there and yet is still getting paid. You can try your hardest, but it's not going to happen. Now, go to a softball game and ask someone wearing a jersey what they're doing there. I can guarantee their response won't be cooking, painting, or looking for the condiments aisle. There is only one "rule" when it comes to teams: to be a member of the team, you must have a function. Meaning if you don't have a function, then you aren't actually a part of that team.

It might not be immediately self-evident how your function fits into the team's goal (the glue that binds you all together), but everyone on the team has one. And only members of that team are eligible to earn roles. Therefore, to become a leader, you must have a functional duty on the team you are trying to lead. It doesn't matter what it is, just as long as you have one.

# Chapter 10
## Common Ground

The drilling. The buzzing. Young children crying out for help. It's no wonder we all fear and loathe the place. With overhead lighting and equipment straight out of a horror movie, it is without a doubt my least favorite thing to do. Now for the record, I brush my teeth, and I even floss occasionally, but still, every time I sit in that sterile plastic recliner, my blood pressure rises like I'm being dropped into a shark tank. To say the least, I'm on edge. But rightfully so—I'm about to go molar to molar with the one person who can single-handedly ruin my whole week—the dentist.

I don't have anything against my actual dentist, per se. I get it, they're just doing their job. Clearly these individuals have some deep-seated psychological issues to choose this line of work, but dentistry is consistently ranked as a top career choice. Not to mention everyone has teeth—making it a pretty solid business model.

Becoming a dentist, although a lot of hard work, is for the most part pretty straightforward. Just about every dentist out there has taken more or less the same path.

- Finish high school—go to undergrad—graduate with a bachelor's degree—go to dental school—graduate with DDS—become dentist

Yes, there can absolutely be deviations along the way (internships, gap years in Thailand, etc.), but the overwhelming majority of dentists will take this route, and as humans, we love this. The steps are clearly defined. It's black and white. If X, then Y. Do this, become that. Follow the steps, go to dental school, become a dentist, buy a yellow Hummer. Straightforward, with little ambiguity or gray space.

In the beginning, a person decides "I want to become a dentist," which kickstarts their journey. It's a conscious decision they make. You'll never find someone that just fell into being a dentist—somebody who was always fascinated by teeth and then eventually just started doing dentistry (weirdo—and also terrifying). Thankfully, that's not how it works. Every dentist out there made a concerted effort to work on teeth. Whether their rationale was an interest in cuspids, a desire to make a good living, or pressure from their parents, all dentists share this same launch point of "I want to become a dentist."

Pick another career off the top of your head and search for it online. "How to become a *(blank)*." I bet it's pretty well defined. Functions are usually like that, with quantifiable steps on how to achieve them; and everyone in that function at one time made the decision to pursue it. Roles are a lot different and trickier to nail down in that respect. Earning a role, specifically the leader role, is usually much less defined.

***

We know that the leader role can be acquired by any functional duty on the team. (Any person on any team has the possibility to become a leader.) With our world broken up into billions of teams, each with its own wide-ranging set of functional duties that comprise it, there's essentially an infinite number of ways the leader role can manifest itself. Can you imagine the flowchart for that? What a mess.

Sometimes you read a book or watch a video where someone describes one very specific path to becoming a leader. It's usually the one they took and they are sharing their journey, and that's great, but don't forget, there are endless ways to earn the leader role. And if theirs doesn't jive with you, your personality, your interests, or your demeanor—that's okay. That was their journey, not yours. There isn't a "one size fits all" for leadership. Thankfully, anyone can do it, and anyone can be great at it.

*\*\**

Warning. This next section comes with a disclaimer.

We are diverging again from our old ways of thinking about leadership. We all have a preexisting condition when it comes to what we have been told a leader is, and what it is great leaders actually do. For this reason, I need you to remember back for a moment to the fictional character, Gumby.

Gumby was kind of a funky dude. Green and made of clay, he could do what you might expect him to—change. In order to achieve success during his thirty-minute missions, he could stretch, shrink, and conform his body into some wild shapes. Like the lost green Avenger, Gumby could become whatever was needed to get the job done. And for this reason, I want you to picture every leader in the world as Gumby.

Countless green humanoids sprinkled across our planet. Clay manikin leaders all walking around with the same morphing powers as Gumby. All the great ones you can think of—all of them now green.

*⁂*

Here is a list of some exceptional leaders (some of my favorites) and a great example of how leaders come in all shapes, sizes, colors, ethnicities, races, sexes, genders, and functional duties. The teams they were a part of varied vastly in composition and structure, but I think we'd all agree (because the leader role is subjective) that they have earned that moniker.

- Martin Luther King Jr.—an American civil rights activist who helped fight racial discrimination and inequality in the 1950s and 1960s through peaceful protests and powerful speeches. He is best remembered for his "I Have a Dream" speech and his participation in the African American civil rights movement.
- Harriet Tubman—an African American abolitionist, humanitarian, and antislavery activist. Born into slavery, she escaped and went on to rescue hundreds of other slaves using the network of antislavery activists and safe houses known as the Underground Railroad.
- Mother Teresa—a Roman Catholic nun and missionary who lived in India and devoted her life to serving

the poor and impoverished around the world. She founded the Missionaries of Charity in Calcutta, India, in 1950 and was awarded the Nobel Peace Prize in 1979 for her humanitarian work. She dedicated her life to caring for the poor, sick, orphaned, and dying, and was canonized as a saint in 2016.

- Mahatma Gandhi—a famous leader of India's independence movement. He was a proponent of non-violence, civil rights, and social justice. He helped lead India to freedom from British rule in 1947 and is often referred to as the father of the nation. He is remembered for his peaceful protest methods, self-sacrifice, and commitment to social justice.
- Abraham Lincoln—the sixteenth president of the United States, serving from 1861–1865. He is best known for leading the country through the Civil War and issuing the Emancipation Proclamation, which eventually led to the freeing of all slaves. He was a strong advocate for democracy and civil rights. He was assassinated in 1865 and is still remembered today as one of the greatest presidents in US history.
- Clara Barton—a pioneering nurse who founded the American Red Cross in 1881. She served as a nurse in the Civil War, distributing supplies and tending to wounded soldiers. She also served as a teacher, a patent clerk, and the first woman to hold a government position. She was an advocate for civil rights and women's rights.
- Susan B. Anthony—an American leader in the early women's suffrage movement. She devoted her life to advocating for gender and racial equality as well as other civil rights issues. She was a key figure in winning the right for women to vote in the US and served as a founding member of the National American Woman Suffrage Association. She is remembered as an iconic figure in the struggle for gender justice.
- John Wooden—an American college basketball coach for the UCLA Bruins from 1948 to 1975. During this period, he amassed an impressive record

of ten NCAA Division I Championships and twenty conference titles, earning him the nickname "The Wizard of Westwood." Wooden was lauded for his commitment to developing his players, as well as his emphasis on hard work and team play.

Now, you might look at this list and think, *What could they all possibly have in common?*—this is a pretty diverse list of folks. Some more jovial, some more serious, some outspoken, and others much more reserved. Hall of Fame–level leaders with what appears to be little in common, and for our purposes, all of them are now Gumby.

The progression of how someone becomes a Gumby is actually pretty straightforward. At its highest and most simple level, it looks like this:

- Person on a team performs actions such that people start seeing them as a leader

And believe it or not, sometimes people who are now Gumby didn't even mean to do it. Becoming a leader was never their intent, which is a giant deviation from how functional duties work. I have known people I absolutely consider to be leaders that I can guarantee never once made the conscious decision to be a great leader. It just happened.

They behaved in a way that, while performing their functional duties, earned them the leader role over time from everyone on the team. Be funny for long enough, and whether you like it or not, people may consider you the class clown. Yes, you can intend to earn the leader role and then set out to become one (probably the reason you're reading this), but you can also "fall into leadership" by doing those same things. So clearly, the desire to become a leader is not a shared starting point among all leaders (unlike dentists). It doesn't matter if you intended to be a leader or not—it is still possible to end up as a Gumby. So, the question remains—what do all leaders have in common?

We need to go up a level.

***

Gandhi, Harriet Tubman, and John Wooden walk into a bar—would obviously be the start of a time-traveling joke because besides being great leaders, they have almost nothing in common. And that's not unique to these three; there's actually not much that leaders across the board share with one another. And when I tell people this, they often give me a funny look. If you put your list of great leaders next to my own personal list, next to five hundred other lists, next to the all-stars I just mentioned—there's not much overlap. Our same brains that love finding patterns through comparison usually fixate on the minutia, the details, the stuff you only see under a microscope. We get hung up on the parts that really don't matter, like demeanor, upbringing, or winning percentage. This is why I wanted you to picture them all as Gumby. Gumby can be anyone. All shapes and sizes. All the functional duties, personalities, beliefs, races, genders, sexes, ethnicities— Gumby (leaders) can be them all. In a literal sense, the only thing that one Gumby shares with another is that they are green and made of clay. And when it comes to real-life leaders, they also have only one thing in common.

The leaders I named are pretty high profile, which makes them easy to look up (if you don't know who any of them are). Keep in mind that if you were to swap out these eight individuals with your own all-star eight, this logic would still hold. Those leaders (like all leaders) earned the leader role within the teams they were a part of. For some their team was a social cause, for others it was an entire nation, and for one it was a team of basketball players. Each team had its own shared goal, and ultimately, achieving it was the only thing those leaders wanted.

That's it—the common ground, and the one thing all Gumbys share. The overarching objective for every leader is for their team to succeed.

- Martin Luther King Jr.'s team goal: gain equality for all men, women, and children of color

- Harriet Tubman's team goal: get enslaved blacks their freedom
- Mother Teresa: provide services for the less fortunate in India
- Mahatma Gandhi: achieve India's independence from Great Britain
- Abraham Lincoln: end slavery and preserve the United States
- Clara Barton: provide medical care during the American Civil War
- Susan B. Anthony: get women the ability to vote in the US
- John Wooden: win the college basketball national championship

Some of these leaders even ended up losing their lives on behalf of their team's goal because of how passionately they worked toward achieving it. It was their singular focus in life, and because of how they led those teams, most of us (sometimes centuries later) know who they are.

Now, this is obviously a special list, but if you did this for your own leaders in your own life, it would produce the same result. Bob DeMeyer was my high school football coach and one of the best leaders I've ever had. He, like the people in the list above and everyone else on earth, is a part of many teams. Three that we shared were our football team, our high school, and the community we lived in.

- Bob DeMeyer—football team goal: win the Wisconsin state high school championship
- Bob DeMeyer—high school team goal: prepare young men and women for the real world
- Bob DeMeyer—community team goal: make our city a better place to live for all residents

On each of these teams, Coach DeMeyer has earned the leader role due to how he has performed his functional duties as a head coach, a teacher, and a citizen—which makes him now Gumby.

The goals of these teams have almost nothing in common. Suffrage and state football championships are about as far apart as you'll ever find. The specific actions these leaders took to earn the leader role have almost nothing in common, nor do the paths each of them took in their leadership journeys. The only thing they, and every leader that has ever walked the planet, share with one another—they simply wanted their teams to succeed.

For some, it was a goal they diligently worked at daily. For others, it consumed their entire being. And it's the only thing all our Gumbys have in common (whether they realize it or not).

Now, simply having this desire does not make you a leader. I need to emphasize that. Just because you want your team to achieve its objectives doesn't mean people will consider you a leader. It takes more than that. You earn a role through your actions and how you perform your duties on that team. But the overarching goal of every leader is the same—their team's success. It shapes their actions and changes how they view their function, but most importantly, it impacts how they interact with others on the team—"I have many goals, but I want nothing more than for this team to succeed."

It's the guiding principle—the North Star—for all leaders. And you can obviously want your team to succeed without ever having the desire to become a leader, which is why so many people grow into one when it was never their intent. Never even on their radar. The engineer working in a cubicle can have team success as their goal just like their manager can, the same way a vice president or the janitor that cleans the hallways could. It doesn't matter what your function is, as long you are actively working toward the success of your team, you now share the one thing that all leaders have in common.

# Chapter 11
## Multiples

I was devastated. Dare I say in shock. "What do you mean I didn't get the part? I'm like the third-grade Denzel. This has to be some sort of error. Let me speak to the casting director." But no mistake had been made, and I was not going to be playing the part of "Doggie, the bartender" in our third-grade rendition of *Wild Bill*. An interesting character to leave in for an elementary production, but a role I somehow felt born to play. Voice inflections, dramatic pauses, fake drink pouring—I had all the tools to make Doggie come to life in our small Wisconsin classroom.

I remember how embarrassed I felt when Ms. Alexovich announced to the class who got what parts. "Thank you everyone for trying out, but there were four people reading for Doggie, and unfortunately there can be only one in the play . . . Joe, you'll be the stagecoach driver." The stagecoach driver—*Excuse me?* I was crushed, but sadly that's just how plays work. There can only be one of each character, making it the polar opposite of how leadership works.

On small teams, it's kind of hard to picture this, so for now let's focus on a large one: the United States in the 1860s. At one point, there were twenty states remaining in the

Union, with a population of 18.5 million people. Abraham Lincoln was the most influential leader on that team, but I think it goes without saying—there were other leaders in the country while he was in office. Yes, the president has a function with a lot of exposure, making them very well known, but there are tons of leaders on a team of that size. Even on a basketball team, there can, and should, be multiple leaders. The Chicago Bulls had Phil Jackson as their coach and leader, but he wasn't the only one. Lesser-known Bulls like Steve Kerr and Bill Paxton were known for their leadership on and off the court as well. It didn't matter that they weren't the best players on the team; they were able to earn the leader role from their teammates because of their actions in pursuit of the team's success. It had nothing to do with how many points per game they scored.

The greatest teams of all time, current or past, have had more than one leader. The very best usually have many, many more. And since there's no requirement for which functions can earn the leader role, it should come as no surprise that multiple individuals can earn this role simultaneously.

And yes, this holds true even at work. In fact, I find it to be especially true in the office. We all have someone with functional authority who presides over us (the facts of life). A common occurrence, and an unfortunate one at that, is when the boss is a poor leader and people start looking to others on the team for guidance, mentorship, or just daily support. Maybe the manager is a jerk and treats people horribly, or maybe they are the absent type and couldn't care less about the members of their team; either way, they've lost all respect. It soon becomes self-evident and well accepted to everyone who the true leaders on the team are (and there are often multiple). However, it doesn't take a bad boss for someone else to earn the leader role.

You can absolutely have a great boss that is a good leader, and have someone else on the team become a leader as well. On small teams, this is sometimes hard to fathom, but it can (and absolutely should) be done. You know how that great boss-leader of yours acts? The stuff that makes you regard them as such a good leader? Well guess what—you can act in a way that earns you the leader role from others at the exact same time your boss is doing it. It's something I don't think is encouraged enough at work, which is unfortunate, because I believe it is directly related to how successful an organization is, or will be in the long run.

***

There are a couple of common sayings I hear on the topic of teams, success, and leadership. I somewhat agree with these, but the flaw here is that the term *leader* is being used as a synonym for *manager* or *boss*.

1.  *People don't leave bad jobs; they leave bad leaders.*
    You can have an incompetent boss who isn't very good at their functional duty of being a manager. Can't delegate, can't come up with a vision for the team, poor at giving feedback, etc. The result is that you will want to leave that team. The boss may treat you great and encourage you at every step of the way, but they are just no good at their actual job, and your team is suffering because of it. Also, it glosses over fair compensation, workplace culture, benefits, and the countless other factors that must align for someone to decide to stay employed by a company. However, I like do like this saying because it emphasizes the impact someone in a managerial position has on the well-being of others. A manager needs to be good at their job and a good leader at the same time, to keep people happy and engaged on the team.

2.  *There are no bad teams, just bad leaders.*
    This one is pretty similar to the first saying, in that you can have a person in a managerial or coaching position that is no good at the functions of their job. The entire team is held back due to their poor decisions. A sports analogy would be a coach calling the wrong plays, using the wrong personnel, or not understanding the nuances of the game. Or it's possible the players on that team simply aren't up

to par for getting the job done, and the manager/ coach hasn't recognized that yet (or they have, and they are too afraid that others will think they are a jerk if they take action to make the team better). Yes, if the manager or coach is a bad leader, it absolutely increases the likelihood of that team losing or being unsuccessful, but usually, the person referenced in this saying (the person in charge) can mess things up in a multitude of ways that can cause the team to suffer.

And although I find issues with them as blanket statements, I'm all for holding those in positions of power accountable for being a good leader (which is what I think those sayings are attempting to do). Not only do these individuals play a direct part in the success of their team, but they also set the tone for everyone and directly impact the well-being of those around them. Having many leaders on one team is one of the best strategies for succeeding as a team or organization. But it begs the question—with all these leaders and bosses running around, who's actually in charge?

# Chapter 12
## Who's in Charge?

"Wow, what a little diva."

"Seriously, who does she think she is?"

"Oh my God, she farted."

Full of emotions, disapproving sighs, and at times excessive gas- anyone that has met her will agree, our dog Polly is a handful. We have an ongoing joke in our house that she's the boss. I'm smiling as I write this because it's so true (really more of a fact of life than a joke at this point). Like many people with animals, my wife and I end up planning most of our day around her. Now, in fairness to Queen Polly, she can't let herself out to use the bathroom, so we have to make sure we're always back in time to do that. But her giant sighs telling us to turn the TV down so she can sleep, or her refusal to walk on wet grass after it's rained, or the way she purposely pees on the sidewalk even when the lawn is available—that's all Polly. Am I partly (fully) to blame for raising her this way from when she a puppy? Absolutely. I'm the first to say that I spoiled Polly rotten. She's so cute, how could I not? However, it's clear to anyone that comes over to our house: this power has gone to little Pol-Pol's head.

Thankfully for us, Polly can't talk, or we would be in for a world of hurt. "Put my blankie on me, give me another treat, look away while I do my business." The demands could get out of hand quickly. We all know where she lands in the hierarchy of our family team, and it's safe to say that usually, it's at the top. Now, of course I jest a bit. Polly is a dog, and ultimately what my wife and I say goes, meaning that in reality, we are the ones with the power in this dynamic. However, in real life, determining "who's in charge" is actually much more complicated and difficult to discern.

***

Everyone likes clarity. In fact, I can't think of anyone that walks around without their glasses on because they enjoy the painful excitement of bumping into things. Only a sick monster would risk stubbing a pinky toe if they didn't have to. Even if the path ahead is laden with Legos and dog toys, making your midnight trek to the bathroom that much more dangerous, it's comforting (and less stressful) to have the lay of the land. We take solace in knowing just how treacherous our future is going to be. When it comes to the structure and hierarchy of a team, our feelings are no different. At the end of the day, everyone wants to know who's in charge. Unfortunately, it's not that simple to decipher, and I must give you an answer you're not going to like—it depends.

For starters, let me ask you—what does it even mean to be in charge? People listen to you? They do what you say? Or maybe—people *have* to listen to you? You say something, and even if they don't want to, it reluctantly gets done?

There's a subtle difference between those, and dissecting them is how we uncover the answer to who is in charge on your teams. And for the record, being in charge is absolutely not the point of this book. However, I've noticed and experienced how foreign this can be for new leaders, so I want to help prepare you for any situation you may encounter. And understanding this concept will shine a floodlight onto where the leader role falls within any team.

*** 

Who's in charge is easy to decipher when the person with functional authority (manager, coach, boss, etc.) is also a great leader. It's a lot less clear when they aren't.

From the moment I accepted my first head coaching position, for better or worse, I was the boss. It was in my title: head coach. And as the head coach, I had the final say on all matters related to our team of players and how to manage the game. Who starts, who sits, the plays we run, the drills we do in practice—it's a long list, and the head coach determines most of it. But it didn't take long for me to realize that I was not the only person the team was looking to for direction.

I had been lucky to step into a coaching position that had a very well-established and veteran team of players already on board. They knew the game, they knew what they were doing, and most importantly—they knew each other. Those guys had spent years building relationships and carving out their roles on that rugby team: a couple of goofballs, a few badasses, and two clearly defined leaders. And what I began to notice during my first few weeks on the job upset me. As someone new to leadership, I was completely unversed in what was actually going on.

As a head coach (or anyone in a position of functional authority), sometimes you have to make decisions that aren't unanimously popular. Changing how the team does something on the field, altering playing time, or simply doing anything else that deviates from the way things used to be done. The standard reaction to change for most is apprehension—a slight brow lift when hearing that something you've done for years is now going to be done differently—and this was true for the players on that team. And what quickly started to happen was that I would give the team direction, and there would be a pause before it was carried out.

At first, I didn't know what was going on, and it frustrated me. Not until the end of my second week did I realize what was happening: they were silently confirming everything I said with their established team leaders—the guys that had a tremendous amount of influence on and off the field. Even though these two gentlemen held no formal power (their functional duty on the team was as a player, just like everyone else), their opinion clearly mattered. For years, the way they had performed their duties had earned them the leader role, and as a result, others looked to them for guidance, and often, marching orders.

I, being naïve at the time and knowing almost nothing about the interaction of leadership with functional authority, took this personally. "Why don't they respect me enough to do what I'm telling them to do?" Close, but not quite, Joe. What I should've been asking was, "How do I get them to consider me worth listening to?"

What I was experiencing is a scenario that most of us live out constantly in our day-to-day lives on the teams we're a part of. A tug-of-war between influence and power.

※※※

Every single team on earth has a power structure. Even if you don't realize or formally acknowledge it, one exists. Now, it's not a bad thing by any means—but it is important to understand since so many new leaders get tangled up when trying to traverse it.

There are fundamentally only two types of teams, and it all comes down to how power is distributed among its members: teams with uniform power structures and those with non-uniform power structures. A great example of a non-uniform power team can be found where you work. Most companies have a well-defined authority construct that, although not usually defined to the decimal point and searchable in a database, is pretty well acknowledged and adhered to by all members of the team. It's often visually represented via a company's org chart. The CEO has the largest share of power, followed by other C-Suite executives (chief something officers). Then come the vice presidents, normally followed by directors, senior managers, managers, and finally the people in the company who are actually getting things done (at my work, this would be the engineers). And among all those individually contributing engineers, there are further divisions of power. (For example, a level 6 engineer has more power than a level 2 engineer.) You may have never thought about it, but I bet this makes sense: "I listen to my boss, and I definitely listen to my boss's boss." This mindset of "Oh crap—my boss's boss's boss is telling me to do something—this is clearly a task I better do" is the epitome of a non-uniform power team.

On all teams (regardless of the power construct), there is a finite amount of power; let's say all of it on a particular team is equal to 100 percent. The CEO might own 20 percent of it, and as you work your way "down" the org, the portions get smaller and smaller. Whenever two people in that team interact, whoever has the largest pizza slice of power is technically the one "in charge." Whether we like what the person has to say or not, they have formal authority over us. Now, that doesn't mean we should blindly do whatever they tell us to—absolutely not. I'm simply stating that someone with a larger slice has more power in that scenario.

The other type of team is the uniform power construct. As the name suggests, all the power on this team is evenly divided across every member of that team. All power pizza slices are exactly the same size. Sometimes people refer to these uniform power teams as having no "real" power in them, when in reality, everyone just has the exact same amount—so it washes out and appears that there is no power to be had. Truly an instance of *Why should I listen to you?* Most transient teams, the ones we flow in and out of on a daily basis, are like this.

The people that visit the same dog park as Polly and me are part of a team with a uniform power balance. Nobody has any formal authority over anyone else while we are there—all power slices are exactly even. There is no boss, or boss's boss, or boss's boss's boss that we may encounter and be forced to listen to. The grocery store is another example of this type of transient uniform power team. No other shoppers, those there with the same goal as me to acquire food, have the functional authority to tell me what to do. There's no organizational chart or hierarchy for us to reference (the employees there have one as part of their company's team, but we as customers do not). We all have the same title of *shopper* while we sort through avocados. Then, once we check out and leave the store, we relinquish our piece of power back to the team that is still there doing their shopping. It gets absorbed and then evenly distributed out to the other shoppers still there—instantaneously. A constant flow happening all the time as people enter and exit. But at every moment, all power is evenly split for everyone in a transient team.

\*\*\*

The amount of power someone has is tied to their functional duties, a.k.a. their title—manager, senior manager, head coach, president—essentially making those power levels fixed in our day-to-day work lives. Sure, we will all at some point in our careers, either get promoted or leave a company for a different job and disrupt (only momentarily) the construct of power on that team, but it isn't an everyday occurrence. I've been a manager with my current team for two years. During those 730 days, I've had the exact same amount of power as when I started on day one. My title has been *systems engineering manager* every day that I've logged on to my computer. My power pizza slice, because it's tied to my functional duties, is like our eighty-pound princess of a dog in the morning—static and immovable.

Even if I choose to act like an absolute jerk to everyone around me—an ass that treats people like disposable objects and has zero empathy, compassion, or respect for other human beings—as long as I don't do anything to have my title removed (fired, demoted, etc.), I will retain my power. Which is absolutely bonkers, but sadly, that's just how it is. Power is static. The slices of pizza on a non-uniform power team (usually those teams associated with generating revenue) are written in concrete, and they are immovable unless a person leaves or their title changes.

There is a senior manager where I work that is the absolute worst. They berate and belittle almost every person they come in contact with. People dread working for them—so much so that employees have had HR and our ethics team investigate them on multiple occasions. Yet, for whatever unknown and mysterious reason, our company has not fired or demoted this individual. Meaning they still have the exact same amount of power as any other senior manager at work. From day one on the job years ago, to now decades later—despite having been an absolute nightmare—their pizza slice remains unchanged.

When this manager gives direction to their team, everyone cringes inside because they know they have to do it—but they definitely don't want to. But this internal dilemma doesn't only happen when someone is a tyrant. In my first two weeks of coaching, I experienced the same thing, although for different reasons. I had power on my team, but that's all I had. There was no other motivation for people to listen to what I was asking them to do. As the head coach, my pizza slice of power was the largest on the team. They had to listen to me. But it was clear they didn't want to.

*\*\**

It's an incredible thing to witness when people choose to listen to someone even though they don't have to. For what could be a host of reasons, they are actively engaging themselves in an act because someone else—someone they clearly respect—asked or told them to. One of the best examples of this is Martin Luther King Jr. during the American civil rights movement. King's formal titles were minister in his church and doctor (PhD) of theology in the academic community. However, during his time supporting the civil rights movement, he held no official title, meaning he didn't have any more power than anyone else did. When King asked for support, people did so because they wanted to, not because they had to.

There was no "civil rights org chart" that told activists who they had to listen to. In fact, the civil rights movement was ultimately a uniform power team. Every member supporting the fight for equality had the exact same amount of power as the person next to them, and they were free to enter and leave the team at any time (a transient team). But people didn't leave. In fact, they did the opposite—they risked their lives for a cause they believed in. Sometimes doing things that would put them directly in harm's way, things that were orchestrated by one of the movement's leaders, Martin Luther King Jr. They carried out these acts not because they had to, but because they wanted to— because Dr. King had earned the leader role from them and had a tremendous amount of influence on the team.

Unfortunately, in our day-to-day lives, we are rarely exposed to this type of leadership excellence—and almost never at work in our non-uniform power teams. Inevitably, there is someone with functional authority over us, and we hope deep down that they are a great leader, so their influence makes it an easy decision to listen to them.

So why do we choose to listen to great leaders and reluctantly comply with what our supervisor tells us to do? Who's in charge at any given moment has everything to do with the human hierarchy of reasons for doing anything—ever—and is what ultimately separates influence from power.

# Chapter 13
## Humans

Last week, I saw someone tilt their head back and projectile sneeze into the air at Home Depot. I've had someone run their shopping cart into the back of my legs at Target, hear me shout in pain, then continue choosing a toothpaste like nothing happened. Just last month, I saw someone pick their nose in line at the post office and rub it on the package they were about to send, like it was no big deal. There are some real twisted sickos out there, and yet for how annoying I sometimes find people, I love being human. Call me a masochist, but I think it's our flaws that make us special, unique, and lovable. You don't fall in love with a robot (yet)—you fall in love with a person. Two legs, opposable thumbs, and the uncanny ability to make life decisions on a gut feeling. If given a do-over, I think I might just choose to be human again (with giant tortoise a close second). And for how complex our day-to-day lives can seem, with the heaps of emotional baggage we all tote around with us every second of every day, we are shockingly simple creatures.

Whether we're popping frozen waffles in the toaster for breakfast, ordering a third rain jacket on Amazon, or reading this book—everything we do has a reason. Something has motivated us to make a decision and then take action. Even if the thing we're doing is absolutely nothing, getting bored out of our minds on the couch, something in our brain prompted us to simply relax. And despite how complicated professors, textbooks, and general education courses may have made this appear in undergrad, everything you've done today can be binned into just two categories.

※※※

As I sit here writing at 6:20 a.m. on a Wednesday, here has been my morning so far: use the restroom, make coffee, drink some water, let Polly out, turn on the news, start writing. A classic start to my day, although on occasion I do live dangerously and switch things up. Often, I'll head to the gym first before working on this book. Sometimes I listen to music and leave the news off. However, a few actions reoccur in all my mornings: use the restroom, drink water, let Polly out. These are not so much choices for me as they are basic requirements, my standard operating procedure. Not things I want to do, but rather things I need to do. And yes, sometimes there is an overlap. I enjoy taking Polly out and starting my morning with some fresh air, but even on the bitterly cold mornings when I could do without the freezing cold winds, she has to go out. That is something I have to do, whether I want to or not.

Another activity I do every weekday is go to work. Whether virtually logging on from home or making the trek in to our absurdly outdated offices, I go to work five days a week. Some mornings I wake up and think to myself, "I really enjoy this job, let's get after it today," while other times it's closer to "This is absolutely horrible and I'd rather be electrocuted for hours than go in today." Either way, it's off to work I go.

On the other end of the spectrum, something I want to do most days because I enjoy it is read a book. Don't get me wrong, I like watching *New Girl*, *Schitt's Creek*, or *The Office*, but after a long day at work, the last thing I want is to look at another screen. So, to keep my eyes from burning into my skull, I turn to the tried-and-true pastime of reading words on pages. I'm not really a fan of fiction, so I usually lean toward a biography or something historical. I'll sit there and read for hours if I'm in the zone. After grabbing a lemon-flavored La Croix and some salt and vinegar chips, I'm off to the races on an activity that brings me pleasure. Certainly not one I have to do during my day, but one I definitely enjoy and try to squeeze in wherever I can.

Here are some other activities (in no particular order) that you may find me doing during the week: going to the gym, feeding Polly, cleaning the kitchen, driving to work, going snowboarding, doing house renovations, making dinner, playing golf, grocery shopping, going on a date with my wife, and so on. Take a moment and make a mental list of your own. What have you been up to lately? Then I want to know, why did you decide to engage in those activities? What inside your brain told you to do each of those? For me, it looks like this:

- Read a book—It's relaxing and stress relieving (something I want to do).
- Feed Polly breakfast—She has to eat to stay alive (something I have to do).
- Clean the kitchen—It's more enjoyable to live in a clean house (want to).
- Drive to work—Everything costs money (have to).
- Go snowboarding—It's a fun and exciting activity (want to).

Without going down a psychology wormhole, at its core, your list is broken down into only two categories. Things you want to do, and things you have to do. That's it. Pretty simple. Now, could you decompose these down further into minute subcategories, using every tool in the psychology playbook? Absolutely. Is that how my brain works? Not at all. I am but a simple creature, and as such, my brain is shockingly uncomplicated.

"What about the things I *should* do, Joe? Where do those go, huh?"

An activity you should do is most often one you have to do; you're just reluctant to do it. If you have actions in the *should* category, ask yourself—what would happen if you just didn't do them? If it's okay that you didn't, then it was a want-to action. If things go to hell because of it not happening, it was a have-to. Which leads me to my next question—how did you pick what goes where?

\*\*\*

Every moment of every day, we are doing things because we either (a) have to do them or (b) want to do them. There really are no other options. And before we get too far, I want to be clear that if we compared our lists, they would be different.

You and I, although a lot alike in our pursuit of better leadership, are very different people. It's obvious, but I feel worth saying out loud—all people are different people. As such, what we lump into have-to and want-to categories will vary from person to person. I have to feed my dog, and you may not even have a pet. Or maybe that is something your partner does. Perhaps we share an activity like working out, which for me is a want-to because I like fitting into my pants, and for you it's a have-to because it is directly tied to your daily mental health. Beyond eating and drinking, I can't say for certain what your list will look like—that's for you to decide. But even though our lists are wildly different, the motivation for each category is always the same:

Level 1: things we have to do—actions that are directly tied to our basic human needs

Level 2: things we want to do—actions related to our wants and desires as humans

\*\*\*

Even though I enjoy (for the most part) what I do at work, there are some pretty tedious parts to my job that really make me reconsider my life choices. I love the people, which is why I got into management as a career, but like most of us in the twenty-first century, I could do without the endless daily email tsunami, or the hours spent working on a PowerPoint chart that will get mere seconds of airtime in my team's next presentation. Things I don't enjoy doing but absolutely have to do because, believe it or not, they are directly tied to my basic needs as a human.

- Submit work presentation—stay employed—continue getting paid—pay mortgage and buy food

Most don't even realize they are making this connection between work and their basic human needs. Thankfully, the urge to survive comes naturally to us. Meaning we are constantly doing this, every moment of every day—making decisions based on our basic Level 1 (L1) needs as a human. All those actions you put into your have-to category got put there instinctively, whether you realized it or not, and are directly tied to your basic needs as a human. Often, these actions are associated with food, water, shelter, and safety. The classics for survival. Not things we want, but rather things we absolutely need. The gotta-have-its. Now, you might look at your list and go, "How does doing *that* relate to my basic needs as a person?" Sometimes it isn't self-evident that something belongs in L1, but if you trace it back upstream, you'll find it eventually flows into the basic needs section.

I have to mow the yard. After a little detective work, you can see why this really is something I am obligated to do.

- Mow the yard: If I don't, the HOA tickets us—HOA eventually puts a lien on our house for being noncompliant—get in trouble with the bank—lose our home

However, our basic needs go well beyond simply staying alive. Things like being appreciated, accepted, and understood also live in Level 1 because we have to have them, and as so many of us have sadly witnessed, our emotional and mental health are matters of life and death. So whatever actions satisfy these needs for each of us get lumped into L1 as well.

- Feed Polly: Without food, Polly will starve. I love Polly, so if something happened to her, I would be devastated. This directly impacts my emotional and mental well-being.

Level 1 needs are things we've determined and cultivated over the course of our lives. No two lists will be the same, but we all share these core tenets: food, water, shelter, safety, emotional and mental wellness. And no matter how you slice it, we need to have these in order to exist.

*\*\**

Level 2 is a magical place. Removed from the basic, life-instilling choices that keep us breathing and upright, Level 2 (L2) is reserved for the things we simply want. Happiness, joy, and success all reside here. Stuff we could absolutely live without, but things that we desire for as humans. Anything on your list of actions that could be removed without serious detriment to your overall existence belongs in L2. Often, it's as simple as "I like it, it makes me happy." Other times it's a bit more nuanced, like wanting to be successful, or famous, or rich. Either way, you don't need this to survive. You just want it to make survival more enjoyable.

- I could definitely survive without a trip to Hawaii—but I do love a good beach.
- I don't have to go snowboarding on chilly winter days, but peel off my neck gaiter and you're going to find my frozen mustache smiling back at you.

- It doesn't take millions of dollars to live a comfortable life, but who wouldn't want to fly private?

We take a lot of actions every day that we don't have to or need to do. That's the epitome of Level 2. Nice to have, but could do without.

Every decision we make, and every action that follows, can be boiled down into satisfying either Level 1 or Level 2. And in order to effectively lead your teams, it's crucial to recognize how these categories interact with one another.

\*\*\*

Believe it or not, I have never peed my pants while reading on the couch.

A statement that goes without saying (I hope). I like reading, but I would never jeopardize my pants, our couch, or the decades-long streak I have of not soiling myself simply because I'm so enthralled in my Winston Churchill biography. When I get the urge to go, I get up and go. Maybe I finish the paragraph or page I'm on, but there comes a point where I am putting that book down one way or another. And if I get that urge and I'm not near a restroom, then just like for everyone else, finding one gets immediately reshuffled to the top of my to-do list.

Likewise, if I'm relaxing on the beach and by some freak accident my glass breaks and slices my finger open, I'm not going to sit there and bleed out while I continue to soak in the sun. No, I'm going to momentarily freak out, apply pressure to the wound, and then calmly find the nearest place where I can get stitched up. No matter how amazing that sunset may be, I will not bleed to death for it. None of us would. It's the same reason nobody is going to die of dehydration while they mindlessly scroll through social media for days. No matter how adorable those baby elephant videos are, they will eventually lose out to our basic needs as a human. Silly examples, but it's so true: we can only stay in Level 2 while our Level 1 needs are being met.

Except it's not always that extreme.

Those examples all had to do with time-critical bodily functions or survival needs. Pretty simple to see how L1 and L2 fall into order there. In real life, during the day-to-day grind, it's rarely this black and white. Especially when those actions are a ways downstream from the instincts we used to place them there. The result is something we're all too familiar with—we switch the order up. Put wants before needs. Success before our own well-being. But we can only sustain this for so long. Eventually, the fourteen-hour workdays catch up to us. We miss enough birthdays, we lose enough hair, and we feel so unappreciated that, in our current situation, we simply cannot continue to be successful (L2).

We've put off L1 for too long, and in doing so sacrificed our mental and emotional well-being for the betterment of our careers. This is often referred to as burnout, but I prefer a different term: erosion. Our foundation gets washed away until we're left floating, suspended momentarily in midair like Wile E. Coyote chasing the Road Runner in Level 2, desperately pursuing something we want (success) without solid ground to stand on. An unsustainable position for anyone to be in.

Maybe it ends in applying for new jobs, maybe in a mental breakdown, perhaps both. But either way, you can't keep going on like that. Despite our best efforts, and whether we are cognizant of it or not, as human beings, we will always strive to restore the correct order. Subconsciously, our primitive brains recognize that basic, life-instilling needs must be met first, and eventually, they will get shuffled to the front.

❊❊❊

It took a minute, but we're here. We can finally answer *Who's in charge?* and see why we have to listen to our bosses even when we don't want to. Even if they're a jerk, one of the most basic rules on a team is that we have to listen to those with more power over us. That's because doing so satisfies our Level 1. For starters, doing what your boss says keeps you safe from discipline. In the Stone Age, this would've put our physical safety in jeopardy; however, today it could certainly lead to getting "called into the principal's office." Most people actively try to avoid these situations—which makes listening to someone with more power than ourselves (our bosses) a safe choice.

The other reason we have to listen to our boss, placing them firmly in charge, is that by doing so, we continue to stay employed. Meaning we keep the money stream flowing into our bank accounts, the same money that pays the rent and buys food. To be defiant puts those basic needs in peril and goes against 2.5 million years of human evolution. This is why defying authority makes us feel so uneasy, and excessively sweaty. Our blood pressure rises as the adrenaline starts to pump because our bodies recognize what is happening—Level 1 has been put in jeopardy—so we instinctively prepare to meet the challenge. We've gone against the grain, and our brains intuitively know that the repercussions could be dire. Our very existence, which is defined by Level 1, has been put in question.

Doing things that maintain the status quo in L1, like listening to the boss, is a safe option. This is why when someone with more power does something that is unethical, illegal, or just plain wrong (or tells us to do it), it's so hard to say no. Our survival instincts say we need to listen to them, which is a travesty because there are disgusting bosses out there who need to be put in their place. As an outsider, when you hear stories like this, you say to yourself, "Why didn't they just tell someone what was going on?" or "Why not just tell that piece of scum to screw off?" But it's not that simple. When you're in that position, with over eighty thousand generations of evolutionary lessons engrained in your head insisting that your existence as a living creature is on the line, it's much harder to say no.

To be clear, I'm not saying we should be listening to everything someone with power over us says—I'm just uncovering why we do it. Why we take orders from certain people, and how the power dynamic within a team actually works. Please, please, please, if someone ever tells you to do something you're not comfortable with, tell someone about it. HR, ethics, a colleague, anyone. It's not an easy thing to do, feeling like we are putting our life on the line, but it's 100 percent necessary to get those people out of their position so they can't do that again. The physiological response we have is implanted in us, but it doesn't have to own us. There are many companies you could work for that would treat you better and take you in a heartbeat—meaning your revenue stream and ability to satisfy Li aren't really in question. Don't settle for environments like the one I just described.

But not all managers or people in power are human feces. Sometimes they're just average folks with more power than us telling us to do things we don't like, but because they are our boss, we are obligated to comply. Maybe we don't respect them because they treat us with indifference. Maybe we've seen them do some shady sh*t. Maybe they're just not a nice person, but also not a terrible one. There are a lot of reasons for feeling this way—compelled to do something (a have-to action) that someone in power has told us to do.

***

It's 10:00 a.m. and I'm working diligently at my desk. In walks my boss, Nancy. Nancy tells me about her vision for the team and some tasks she is going to need my help with.

I do what Nancy asks me to.

It's impossible to tell from this vague statement whether I did it because I respect Nancy and she has earned a level of influence with me, or whether I acted because I had to, simply because Nancy is in a position of power over me. The rationale behind "do" in that sentence determines whether Nancy is a leader or not.

# Chapter 14
## The F-Word

In a dark field late at night stands a man. Medium size, average build, with a run-of-the-mill jawline—there is nothing out of the ordinary about this particular specimen. We don't know the events that led to Frank walking through an open pasture in the middle of a crisp fall night, but here he finds himself, staring up at the stars, pondering life, and wondering who's still going to Burger King. Then suddenly he spots something. A bird? Obviously no—it's dark and they're asleep. A plane? Possibly. It's too far away to tell, but it's slowly growing larger in the distance. He's not sure what it is, but it's definitely coming his way.

Instead of running for the treeline like a regular person, he just stands there. Curious, cold, and still full from dinner—his feet are anchored to the ground. As the light approaches, he starts to make out the structure producing the intense glow. It's a craft. Shiny and disk-shaped, a classic blockbuster UFO. But sadly for Frank, who until recently didn't have the internet or basic cable, there is nobody around to warn him of his impending doom, so he stands there awestruck and dumbfounded, hands by his sides, as the giant craft quietly positions itself overhead.

Without any warning, a door slides open from the bottom of the ship and a powerful green light illuminates Frank. He feels himself go weightless and start to inch off the ground. Flailing his arms and legs like a dog learning to swim, he is powerless against the alien tractor beam. Fighting with all his might, he slowly gets pulled up into the ship. The door slides closed, the ship zooms off, and Frank is gone forever.

In its truest sense, this is an abduction. Frank, minding his own business on a dew-covered field, was taken by aliens, never to be seen again. And like most extraterrestrial encounters, there wasn't really an option of whether he would be going along with them. The door opened, the tractor beam engaged, and off Frank went, pulled upward into the night sky. It almost makes you feel bad for the guy. Nobody deserves to be lost forever in outer space, especially when it's something they never asked for. Now, had the aliens gotten out of their ship and presented Frank with options, letting him decide for himself, well, that would make this a completely different story. "Hey Frankie, why don't you come along with us? It's actually pretty fun. Some of these other planets really rage on the weekend. Want to hop on?" To anyone who is presented with that choice and willingly—all on their own—jumps through the open UFO doors—good luck, I no longer feel bad about it. Making the choice to follow the aliens, versus being forcefully sucked up, are two completely different scenarios.

\*\*\*

As rare as alien encounters are, we actually experience this phenomenon all the time. Minus the green light, we are constantly being pushed, pulled, and corralled in directions we did not choose. Complying with what our boss says to maintain Li is the epitome of this. We don't have a choice to deviate or follow another direction since that person has more power than us. Even if we 100 percent do not want to go along with them—we kind of have to. A manager tractor beam that ensures we go wherever they go, that we comply with what they tell us to do.

The word for this is *obey*. "You go where I go because I'm the boss." There's not much free will in the decisions we make when a power construct is engaged. To say we are following someone into their alien ship—while in that moment being sucked up and forcibly lifted off the ground by a mysterious green light—would be misleading. That's because the word *follow* really is the only one like it. And once you understand what it means to follow, the rest of leadership becomes ridiculously simple to understand.

\*\*\*

If I go to my car right now, and you go where I go because you want to be where I am, that's called—creepy. And, following. You're choosing to go where I am. You're *following* me. I'm certainly not forcing you to do this, and I didn't say, "Meet me at my car, or else." No, this was a decision you made. For whatever reason inside your head, you determined that you wanted to be where I was—then actively carried out the action to be there as well, which is what makes this word so unique (and misunderstood).

The word *follow* indicates that a free-will decision has occurred. A choice was made—to go where someone else is (in a classic sense of the word) or to purposely do something in alignment with another's wishes. Not because we are being forced to, but because we are choosing to. No ultimatums, power constructs, or green lights from the heavens coercing us. You don't say "Little Amy is following me" as you pull her behind you with one of those toddler leashes. It wouldn't make sense because that's not following. It's really strange—and you should absolutely judge parents that do this—but it's definitely not following.

Yet this is how we've grown to use the word. Anytime a person goes somewhere or does something in alignment with another's wishes, regardless of why, we say they are following. Even if in reality there is a transparent, silent, and ominous tractor beam forcing them to do so. "Follow the rules" is a great example of this. The rules are, well, the rules. Sure, you can break them (badass alert), but you run the same risks as when you disobey your boss or fail to comply with the law (Level 1 gets put in jeopardy).

I do what Nancy asks me to. Which is the same as "I go where Nancy goes." But why? Was I threatened with urinal duty if I didn't? Am I not going to get paid if I deviate from the path Nancy has so kindly laid out for me? It's hard to tell when we know so little about that interaction. Let's replace "do" with a more descriptive verb.

I follow Nancy. Or, I obey Nancy. Two very different constructs. And we can tell a lot about this dynamic based on the word used. When you hear *follow*, you immediately think, "That's weird. Please be careful, Nancy." But in reality, we follow people all the time. Sometimes in a classic sense, but it usually means going along with another person's vision, example, or request. Following their wishes, not so much their GPS coordinates.

When you hear "I obey Nancy," you go "Ohhhhhh, okay. Joe didn't really have a say in the matter." We obey orders, the law, and commands from those on our teams that have more functional authority than we do. Whichever country you are a citizen of, you are a part of that team. It's commonplace to say "Obey the law." It doesn't freak us out because it's well accepted that laws must be obeyed. Don't rob banks. Pay your taxes. Jaywalk, but only when nobody's looking. Actions that we are commanded to do, or not to do, because our team said so. However, in our day-to-day lives, even in situations that are essentially the same (where we are being forced to do something), we rarely use the term *obey*. Even when it is the best choice for describing the situation.

It sounds off. It makes us cringe. "Obey? No-no-no, you don't to have to *obey* me, that makes me sound like a tyrant. You just have to do what I say, or else you'll be fired and not be able to pay your bills anymore . . ." The ability to choose whether to do something (which is fundamentally what the word *follow* means) is a powerful thing, and it's the reason leadership is such a unique (and confusing) topic. Sadly, most people practicing, studying, or teaching leadership don't recognize this distinction—which stinks because it's the reason regular people (you and I) can become extraordinary leaders.

\*\*\*

The confusion of formal titles and roles, mixed with a fundamental misunderstanding of what it means to follow, has led to this—absolutely wrong—line of reasoning.

*Once I apply to a functional duty that has formal authority tied to it, I automatically become a leader (wrong), and leaders have followers (true). Therefore, when I tell people to do something and they do it, they are following me (wrong). If I go somewhere and my team does too—they must have followed me (wrong). They're my followers; I gained them when I applied for the job (wrong).*

Completely wrong. Yes, leaders have followers, but the leader role is something that has to be earned, meaning you can't inherit followers when you get hired to a functional duty like manager. As much as it pains me to say it, a great example of how this word is supposed to be used can be found from the most pointless thing on earth: social media.

Pick your favorite platform (I'll date myself and use Myspace). As one creates, shares, or engages with content, other people start to take notice. "I like what Becky is doing over there. Good mix of funny and serious, solid rotation of dog pics, more of that would be great," and so they follow Becky. Maybe Becky gets slightly famous from her corgi shenanigans and wakes up one Sunday morning to find that she has amassed 3 million followers. People who, of their own choosing, are keeping up with what Becky is doing. She didn't go to all 3 million houses with a bug zapper and threaten everyone, shouting, "Follow my account, or else." No, every single one of those people did that of their own accord. And even with how much I despise social media, these platforms are using the word to perfection. Building a following is exactly how it sounds. You do things, and people decide to follow you. Well done, Tik-gram-book.

But this behavior isn't just reserved for social media content. We follow people all the time. So, the question remains—why would someone choose to follow someone else?

# Chapter 15
## Why We Follow

"Wilson! WILSON!"

A man lost at sea, watching his only friend slowly drift away into the vast Pacific Ocean. It's an iconic scene and one that strangely breaks your heart. Tom Hanks, bobbing up and down on his makeshift raft, screaming out to what has been his only friend while stranded on a deserted island—a Wilson volleyball with a handprint for a face. *Cast Away* is one of those classic movies that know how to tug at your heartstrings. Tom Hanks plays a regular guy thrown into a survival situation alone, untrained, and without any help, fighting for his life any way he knows how.

There's a moment as Wilson's tiny little face drifts away that you think to yourself, "Would I actually jump in and risk my life to save it?" A few seconds later, it's quickly erased with "No, of course not, because Wilson is just a silly volleyball." But I guarantee anyone who has sat through *Cast Away* feels something as Wilson and Tom say their goodbyes, which I argue is completely normal.

For 143 minutes, we watch Tom Hanks (portraying a character, but he's always Tom to me) struggle to survive for years on an island, during which time the only "person" he can turn to for mental and emotional support is a volley-ball. We see Tom painfully learn how to make fire, spear fish, and apply self-dentistry via an ice skate. Completely untrained and in no way prepared to enter a survival situa-tion—the learning curve is steep, as it would be for any one of us. Thankfully for Tom, he slowly starts to figure things out. But in the beginning, it's painfully rough.

Through no fault of his own, Tom doesn't know how to hunt or gather food. And why would he? He was alive in the twentieth century. A time in history when grocery stores were commonplace. Feeling hungry? Just hop in your car, drive to the closest one, and pick out a dozen glazed doughnuts. Easy. Back in the day though, before civiliza-tion and amenities like running water and delivery food services, this was not the case (as Tom quickly finds out). It was harder to come by food. You had to proactively acquire it by either pulling it out of the ground or hunting some-thing to use its meat for energy. During Tom's first days on the island, as he fails repeatedly at these tasks, we all start to wonder: Would I be able to do it?

For some, the answer is yes. Eventually, after much trial and error (and many hungry nights), we would sur-vive. Maybe not thrive, but we'd get by in agony on stewed slugs long enough to learn from our mistakes and eventu-ally become proficient in our survival skills. Emaciated and cold, but alive. For others, the answer is sadly no, not even close. I don't mean to be harsh, but keeping yourself alive was hard back in the day. One wrong step, one wrong wild mushroom, one failed attempt to warm ourselves after a late-night ocean dip could spell lights out for good. With no YouTube videos at our disposal on "how to spearfish," we would be royally screwed. But what if—by some miracle—there was someone on that deserted island that we could turn to for help? How would that change things?

Say we're sitting on a rock at the beach and see someone down the coast fishing. And not just fishing, but successfully fishing—otherwise known as catching. Stacks on stacks of fish. Big fish, blue fish, meaty fish, sushi fish. Signs that this individual is absolutely dominating the game of survival.

What then? Do we continue sitting there on our rock and turn away from this master class in survival? Starving and on death's doorstep—completely disinterested in what they potentially have to offer? No way, José. Because that would mean going against every fiber in our human bodies telling us to survive.

\*\*\*

Some brave souls walk over immediately and introduce themselves, hoping that this expert hunter is friendly. Others sit there and silently watch their technique from afar, squinting to get every action into focus, all the while gaining insights on how to effectively catch dinner. Either way, we take notice of what Casey the hunter is doing.

We start sharpening our spears like Casey. We start diving into the water like Casey. If Casey has a hairstyle, we might even copy that too—anything to possibly put us in a better position to survive. Most importantly though, we start going where Casey goes because we have a basic need that must be met, and we know they can help us with it. Meaning if Casey picks up shop and moves to the next river over, you better believe we grab our things and do the same.

And we don't care about Casey's status, what their title on the island is, or how much power they have on any of their teams. We simply know that we have a basic need that requires attention, and that by following Casey, we put ourselves in a better position to satisfy it. I need to survive, I need food, I need to pay attention to how Casey fishes and where Casey goes.

Thankfully, we rarely find ourselves on deserted islands. But this same logic holds in our day-to-day lives. The reason we follow someone comes back to why we do anything ever: satisfying our basic needs (L1) or our wants and desires (L2). If we can't do this on our own, or we want support in achieving them, every one of us will search out ways—and people—to help us. Whether we realize we're doing it or not, we are constantly finding ourselves a Casey.

\*\*\*

For as awesome and badass as island Casey sounds, I have yet to follow someone because of their hunting or gathering skills in real life. Our day-to-day lives are usually full of actions that are a bit downstream from how they fit into L1 and L2. Getting food requires making money. Making money requires having a job. Keeping a job requires performing your duties at work. Performing your duties at work requires a safe environment and good mental health in order to be successful. In this instance, Casey takes on a different form.

Maybe they're a manager that's always willing to be flexible when life events pop up and we have to shift our schedule. Maybe they're a coworker who is always asking how we're doing and offering to lend a hand. Maybe it's someone in our office that is quick to stop toxic conversations and always sticks up for people in meetings (even if it puts them in the hot seat). Casey can take on a lot of forms, but rest assured, we all have Caseys in our lives.

The first time I encountered a workplace Casey was as a new graduate in my first job, at a time when I had absolutely no idea what I was doing. My boss was one of those classic absentee managers that you spoke to every other month for five minutes, and who couldn't care less about you as an employee, or a person. I quickly realized that to perform my job duties (and ultimately satisfy my Level 1 needs), I was going to require some help—a little guidance—as I got up to speed.

Luckily for me, Casey was easy to find. She had a reputation that preceded her. Once, when I was discussing a problem I was stuck on, someone mentioned her name to me. "You know who you should really talk to? Casey. She's wicked smart and super approachable." So I got up, walked over to Casey's office, and introduced myself. We chatted for a bit, discussed my engineering question, and as I was about to leave, I got my first hint as to why Casey was indeed a Casey: "And Joe, please don't hesitate to reach out the next time you need help. My door is always open." And she actually meant it.

Everyone in our office knew about Casey. She wasn't a manager and she didn't have much formal power, yet she still set the tone for the entire office. If you had a problem, you went to her. If you needed advice, you went to her. People did what Casey said, even though they didn't have to. Casey was great at being a software engineer, but that's not why we kept following her. Casey was great at her job, but—more importantly—she cared about people being successful at theirs too. She understood that for the team to be successful, I, a hopelessly lost new graduate engineer, needed to be successful. It didn't matter that next to her name in meetings it said *engineer* and not *manager*. We didn't care one bit what her title was. All we knew was that Casey was someone you could turn to for help.

Now, if you approached the expert fisher on the beach and were told, "Stay away from me or I'll send this spear through your shin bone," this would obviously not be someone you wanted to follow. Sure, they're an expert at their craft, but they clearly don't care about the needs of others. Likewise, the fact that our office Casey was an expert in her field had nothing to do with us following her. If she had been a genius engineer but also a pompous, arrogant, know-it-all jerk, well, I doubt any of us would've come through her office door a second time. Thankfully for us, Casey wasn't any of those things, so we kept following her.

***

Caseys don't just appear at work or when we're starving. Our lives are actually littered with Caseys—people we are actively choosing to follow. Although it's a choice we make, it's usually a subconscious decision and not one we weigh out with a pros and cons list. Since *to follow* is directly linked to our human rationale for doing anything ever, our *Homo sapien* brains handle this automatically for us. We know our needs and our wants; they're engrained in us, and without much difficulty, we're able to identify a path for them to be satisfied.

But often, the decision to follow someone isn't related to one specific need or want. Usually, the Casey we identify can lend support across multiple fronts—a variety of our Levels 1 and 2—which makes following them a true no-brainer. We want to be emotionally safe and understood, but we also want to be successful and advance our skills to become more effective members of the team. The more boxes someone checks for us in this pursuit, the more likely we are to decide "This person is a Casey—and someone I want to follow."

In your own life, are there any people you willingly follow? People whose example, teachings, or support you are actively emulating or seeking out? Here are a few of my own. If we compared lists, I bet we would share a lot of the same rationale and logic for why we've chosen to follow someone.

- Casey = my high school head football coach, Bob DeMeyer. He was incredible at providing guidance on how to be a successful player (L2), but he never forgot that my teammates and I were young men, still growing up and preparing to enter the real world. We had homework, exams, work schedules, and other needs (L1) as high schoolers that he always asked about, and he would lend support (mainly flexibility and encouragement) where applicable.
- Casey = my current boss, Amy. Amy is a rarity in the corporate world, a manager that truly cares about the well-being of her employees (L1). She's always asking us how we are and encouraging us to take time away when real-life matters require our attention. Amy also encourages and motivates the team every chance she gets (L2), which is why so many people have told her that if she left the team, they would go as well.
- Casey = author, professor, and TED speaker Brené Brown. Dr. Brown's talk on the power of vulnerability, as well as her books on leadership (*Dare to Lead*

being an excellent example), fundamentally shifted the way leaders are thought of today. Although I do not know Dr. Brown, her teachings and the example she has set for the members of our broader leadership teaching team make her someone I continue to follow.

- Casey = my mom and dad. My parents were exactly what you'd ask for if given the chance to pick your own. I sometimes tell people how supportive or encouraging they were when I was growing up, and I'm immediately reminded, "You know that isn't the norm, right?" They were the classic "You can do it, Joey, and we want to help" type of parents. They didn't spoil me and give in to my every request, but they absolutely put my well-being and potential to be successful at the forefront of their own lives (and I'm forever grateful to them for that).

Upon further inspection, you'll notice that three trends emerge. The first is that Casey is always a member of our team. Coach DeMeyer—Superior High School football team. Brené Brown—leadership teaching community. Amy—my engineering organization. My parents—my family. In every instance, Casey and I were (or still are) part of the same team. The team's size and structure varied greatly, but Casey was always a member.

The second and slightly more confusing discovery, is that sometimes we have never met or spoken directly to our Casey. Weird, right? Well, it's more common than you might first think. It's important to remember the size of some of the teams we are a part of. A football team has one hundred people. The immediate office team we interact with at work might be fifty to sixty, the types of teams where we have direct contact with everyone on it. But it's important to remember that we are all part of some extremely large teams as well.

I'm a member of the United States team (330,000,000), the state of Colorado team (5,800,000), the company I work for team (105,000), and other large teams that don't keep a head count (the leadership teaching community would be an example: extremely large, no idea how many members there are). All things considered, it's sort of incredible that we do this—choose to follow someone even if we have never, and will never, meet them in person. Never once hold a conversation with them. Never give or receive a crisp high five. Only through that person's words and actions (which we received secondhand) did we determine that we're gaining something out of that relationship, and so we keep following them.

The last thing you'll find from your list of Caseys is that we absolutely do not care what Casey's title is on the team. Casey could be a maintenance worker, a librarian, an associate manager, or just another lost soul in the cereal aisle—it doesn't matter. When we decide to follow someone, we are making that choice based on our own needs and wants. Once we identify someone that can help, our brains flick on the follow switch. There's no scrolling through the team roster to find what this person's credentials are. We don't look them up on LinkedIn first to see where they went to school. No, our primitive brains won't allow it. "Me have need, me have want, you can help, I follow you." Titles are fun. Titles are cute. These days everyone has a very long and impressive one, but they don't matter when it comes to being a Casey, which means that the amount of power they have doesn't matter either.

Sounding familiar? I think it's time.

All those Caseys in your life, the people you are following—I want you to picture them now as green clay Gumbys. That's right, tricky me—we've been using Casey as a synonym for a leader this whole time (perhaps you already put that together). Which means if you're only going to remember one thing from this chapter, please make it this:

All followers are volunteers. The people they choose to follow are leaders.

# Chapter 16
## This Is Leadership

Groundbreaking, earth-shattering, and shockingly uneventful is how I would describe it looking back. Nothing special happened to me when this thought came to me—that leaders are just people we choose to follow. In fact, there was no sign at all. An owl didn't land on my balcony and stare into my soul, lightning didn't strike the clock tower across the street, and I didn't find piles of forgotten Bitcoin on my computer. In all actuality, it was pretty uneventful. I was sitting on my overpriced apartment balcony, yet again staring at a blank piece of paper. My goal was simple: define leadership. Do what appeared to be impossible: come up with a short and shareable explanation for it. Something that could easily be given to other people.

Having asked around and seen the distress incurred by this straightforward task, I was beginning to think that maybe it was impossible. Maybe leadership is an enigma. Maybe I should give up and get another ice cream sandwich.

It didn't make sense. If Einstein could describe our entire physical universe with an equation containing only two variables and the speed of light ($E = mc^2$), how was it that leadership required pages and pages of words to explain?

Was leadership more complicated than the principle that governs our very existence? It was starting to seem that way.

Then suddenly, something happened.

I'd like to say the breakthrough that led to this book was due to my oversized cranium lugging around an enormous brain. That I'm actually a pocket genius who has been solving life's mysteries on the daily now for years. But sadly, I am not. My large head has only ever resulted in the need for large hats. But on this day, as I overlooked the sunny parking with a coffee now too cold to drink, I had a thought so outrageous, so far-fetched, so potentially stupid that it just might work. Maybe leadership is better expressed as an equation, not a definition.

I drew, and I drew, and I drew. Letters, shapes, smiley faces—all the things. Erasing, scribbling, crumpling up paper. I didn't know exactly what I was looking for, just that I would know it when I saw it. Neighbors walking their dogs probably thought, "Oh look, honey, that guy must be an architect sketching outside on this beautiful Saturday morning." Wrong. Just a madman trying to find the secret to leadership.

Then, out of nowhere, I wrote down something so simple, yet so shockingly accurate to what I was trying to convey, that I knew I had found it.

At first, I stared at it. I was in denial—no-no-no, this can't be. I wasn't a leadership expert. I didn't have YouTube videos with millions of views, and I wasn't an established leadership speaker charging thousands of dollars for moments of my time. I was (and still am) just a regular guy. My fast-food order is wrong 80 percent of the time, the national average. I have to take my shoes off at the airport. When I point to things, dogs don't understand what I'm doing. I'm the most normal of normal, which is why I think this just might be the ticket to finally understanding leadership. It didn't take a genius to come up with it. Meaning it doesn't take a genius to understand it (no offense).

For some people, this concept takes thousands of words to describe. I argue it can be explained in three characters. This is without a doubt the best-kept secret I could ever share with you.

This is leadership:

$$\blacksquare \rightarrow \odot$$

Someone following someone else. This dynamic. That arrow.

***

The first thing you'll notice is that the arrow from ■ to ⊙ is just that, an arrow. ■ isn't being pulled, coerced, or forced to obey ⊙. In fact, it's quite the opposite. There's an open arrow between the two, indicating that ■ is actively going where ⊙ goes. In this two-dimensional world, if ⊙ started moving up the page, it would look like this:

⊙
↑
■

Down the page, you'd see this:

■
↓
⊙

However, if ■ decided that ⊙ was not someone they wanted to follow anymore, that they weren't getting their Levels 1 or 2 met by following this person, then our graphic would look like this: ■ ⊙. And shortly after, this: ← ■ ⊙

Think back to the list of leaders I had you conjure up earlier. Everyone on your list was an individual you were following—either their teachings, their direction, or their mission in life. In every instance, you and that person were in a leadership dynamic ■ → ⊙. Maybe ⊙ was someone you spoke to on a regular basis, or maybe you'd never met, but either way, there was an arrow from you to them. They didn't have the functional title of a *leader* on your team, but you absolutely considered this person to be one.

In contrast, think of a boss you've had that was a terrible leader. Someone you wouldn't stay late for, someone that you know for a fact didn't care about you as a human. In all those cases, the arrow was glaringly absent.

If I were to sum up the differences between leadership and management graphically, it would be as follows:

This is leadership: ■ → ☉
This is management: [ ■ ☉ ]

With management, there isn't really a choice. ■ is bound to ☉ by that person's power over them. In this 2D world, when ☉ moves, so does ■. Up the page, down the page, left and right, you name it—but the reason is that ■ has to, not because they want to. There isn't any other option. They have to obey, or else they put L1 in question. Being pulled around is not the same thing as following someone. And if you're lucky enough to have a boss you consider to be a leader, it looks like this [ ■ → ☉ ]. Ultimately, leadership is just someone following someone else. The people we choose to follow are leaders.

***

It's so simple, yet we struggle so mightily to communicate this relationship. Following is a choice, which is what makes leadership so special (and until now, difficult to convey). The entire dynamic is predicated on one inconspicuous arrow (→). Facilitating and growing that arrow makes you a leader. Unfortunately, most books, classes, and leadership programs focus on ☉ and all but neglect ■. They provide theories and methods focused on functional duties like knowing how to delegate or come up with a strategic vision, but these have almost nothing to do with establishing the arrow.

It isn't clear then how → is established, or that it even exists at all. This is why many first-timers get confused, thinking that becoming a leader is all about them ☉, when in reality it's all about the dynamic, which doesn't exist without ■. In its truest and most basic sense, leadership is just someone following someone else. ■ following ⊙, because they want to. Establishing and maintaining that relationship means you're a leader. It really is that simple.

# Chapter 17
## The Theory of Leader Relativity

For thousands of years, humans danced around the idea that there were small elemental pieces of matter that made up our world. There was a lot of disagreement on what these fundamental materials truly were (some theories were outrageous), but it was well accepted that you could break down objects in our universe into exceedingly smaller chunks. I'll bypass a long and boring history on the incremental steps and discoveries that led to this, but one day, looking through a high-powered microscope, it was finally laid to rest what we, and everything else in the cosmos, are actually made of—atoms.

Protons, neutrons, and electrons—the building blocks of our existence. They differentiate gold bars from candy bars, and the smell of cookies from poisonous gas. Ridiculously small, impossible to see with the naked eye, and usually taken for granted. The page you're reading right now—atoms. The chair you're sitting on—atoms. Your fingernail polish or mustache wax—you guessed it—bunches and bunches of atoms, working in concert to form everything there ever was and ever will be.

Thankfully, from our zoomed-out vantage point, we can't see the intricacies going on inside an atom (it would probably be disorienting to witness). Though because of that, we're too far away to recognize just how special this construct is. Protons adhering to neutrons, electrons zooming around them, the strong and negative forces at work. It's not until we get up close and personal that we start to see just how special an atom is. I would argue that leadership is the same way.

If you were able to grab onto ■ → ☉ and hold it under a microscope, you would see something magical happening. An intricate dance between leader and follower. Each playing their own part to ensure that this leadership atom is maintained. But like protons, neutrons, and electrons, the two people in a leadership atom are often blissfully unaware of what is happening. It's exceedingly rare to find a detailed plan by both parties to establish and maintain ■ → ☉; it just kind of happens. In fact, both people are usually ignorant of the fact that it is occurring at all. It's not like a light pops up over both their heads and a neon arrow appears out of the clouds. That would be pretty cool, but it's not at all what happens.

■ just knows that they have needs and wants, and that by following ☉ they are in a better position to have them met. ☉ wants their team to succeed and, to accomplish this, is supportive of ■. This rationale is the governing principle that establishes and maintains all leadership dynamics there have ever been and ever will be. It's the basis of leadership and the one thing all great leaders live by, except most have no idea they're even doing it. It's the foundation behind every ■ → ☉, and it's what I now call Leader Relativity.

Looking at leadership ■ → ☉ going from right to left:
- Leaders want their teams to succeed.
- Teams are made of people.
- When people succeed, teams succeed.
- ☉ sets out to ensure everyone can be successful and stay in $L_2$, recognizing that people can only stay in $L_2$ if $L_1$ is being met.

This time, let's start from the other end. Going from left to right:

- People on the team want to succeed.
- But before they can get to and stay in L2, they must have their L1 needs met since they are not capable of succeeding until that happens.
- ■ recognizes that they are better off with the support of ⊙ and decides to follow them.

Leadership is relative to who you are in this relationship. As ■, you see ⊙ as someone who is there to help you meet your basic needs, as well as encourage, empower, and inspire you to be a successful member of the team. Thus, you choose to follow them. As ⊙, you see ■ as a member of your team that is crucial to its success. However, you also realize that they are a complex human and not just a chess piece to be moved and exploited. A person with basic human needs that must be met in order for them to get into, and stay in, Level 2.

This is where I see so many managers, bosses, and functional authority figures get trapped. They desperately want their teams to succeed, but they don't spend time cultivating the arrow (→) "We need results now. Nothing else matters." So they push their people to the limit, treating them like machines. Bad leaders fail to recognize that their team's success (and thereby their own as a leader) hinges on the success of the individuals that comprise the team. And every one of them is a person with real-life needs and wants—and a human-nature hierarchy that dictates every aspect of their daily lives.

Successfully contributing to any team requires hanging out in Level 2 for extended periods of time, which means people are physically unable to succeed before their basic needs are met. You don't binge Netflix while you're bleeding out from a cutlery wound, you won't starve to death while endlessly watching makeup tutorials, and you can't produce for your team while the rest of your life crumbles away.

✳✳✳

You're here because you want to be a great leader. How you go about achieving that will be on a case-by-case basis (which we will get to), but at a high level, this logic flow will guide and dictate how effective you are in this pursuit.

My goal is for our team to succeed.

Teams are made of people.

The people on our team must succeed in order for that to happen.

Our team is full of individuals.

I want Sally to succeed.

I know that Sally, like all people, must satisfy her own L1 before she can be successful in L2.

I care about Sally and her overall well-being.

I say and do things to help Sally.

It sounds almost silly to say out loud—"Caring about people is crucial to leadership"—but it really is. Think about the great leaders you've had in your life. Do you think they understood you as a person? Did you matter to them? Would they go out of their way to help you? One hundred percent yes. And even if that leader was someone you've never met, you still felt like they cared about you as a human. Through their actions or words, which may have never been done or spoken directly to you, there was an understanding that this person actually cared about your well-being.

There will never be someone at the other end of this arrow that makes you feel small, stupid, or unimportant, because why would you willingly follow that person? All the power in the world can't make us follow someone we don't want to. We have to do what our boss says whether they are a good leader or not. But no matter how much power, money, or status a person has, following (→) is a decision that every ■ makes on their own. But it doesn't just happen out of the blue.

***

There's a great scene in *The Office* where Michael Scott and Jim Halpert have switched jobs, with Jim now functioning as the manager and Michael back to working in sales.

Michael, used to his cushy life as the manager where he did basically nothing, is sitting at his desk waiting for the calls (and money) to roll in. Jim grabs his phone and dials Michael.

"This is Michael Scott, Dunder Mifflin," he answers.

"You gotta do something, man, you can't just sit there," Jim replies. And Jim is right. Sales don't miraculously happen. There will never be a line outside your door of people fighting to get in and give you their money. Sales take work. Being a great leader is eerily similar.

Wishful thinkers make crappy leaders. I love telling people this because of the shocked look they give me, but it's so true. Leadership scholars are also not leaders. Don't get me wrong, they can be, but there is no number of books or TED Talks you can watch that will make you a leader in the eyes of someone else. Ten leadership books do not equal one arrow. Nor do a million. Arrows between leaders and followers are created—built from the ground up—and no matter how hard you may wish for them to appear, they won't unless you build them.

My needs and wants are rarely met by someone sitting alone at their desk quietly typing away. Drawn-out email chains do not spark my subconscious mind into thinking, "Now there is someone I should be following." It doesn't work that way. Being a leader—building the arrow and becoming someone others want to follow—takes work. You have to take action to create this dynamic between yourself and someone else.

# Chapter 18
## Arrow Prep

I love pizza. I love almost all kinds of pizza. In fact, I have a real hard time trusting people who *don't* like pizza. Cheesy, saucy, crusty goodness with almost an infinite number of other foods that can be used as toppings—it's no wonder why millions of these Italian pies are consumed every year. And in my long career of eating pizzas, I've had just about every kind you can think of.

Pizzas with vegetables, pizzas with duck, even pizzas with gluten-free crust; put it in front of me and it will get eaten. The only regret I ever feel (apart from all the dairy) is the indescribable pain of biting into a smoking hot slice fresh out of the oven. As it scorches my tongue and leaves permanent damage to the roof of my mouth, I can't help but think, "Why didn't I just wait just one minute before diving in?" Why was I, as I always am, in such a rush to eat this slice of delicious hot lava? It takes sixty seconds—a touch of patience. But no, I am dumb, and this is what I get. Elvis said it best: only fools rush in.

\*\*\*

At this point, you are probably ready to burn rubber and go "be a leader." To slam this book down on your coffee table or launch it out the window, kick open your front door, and go do leadership *stuff.* And I don't blame you. Being a leader to someone else is exciting, and in my mind, it's one of the most rewarding things a person can ever do. But we need to chat a bit about these arrows before I set you loose. Without a proper understanding of how they work, attempting to build them would be like ordering the spiciest burrito at a restaurant you've never been to—*no bueno.*

\*\*\*

So far, leadership (this dynamic: ■ → ⊙) has lived in print on these pages. A two-dimensional representation of a complex, and very real, relationship that occurs between two people. It was designed to be simple on purpose, so that we can more easily explain and share what has up until now been an enigma. However, moving forward, I'd like you to think of these arrows as something you can grab onto. Something tangible that you're able to pick up and touch. An object that if you backed into it on the driveway would raise your insurance premium. A real-life thing with density and mass.

That's because on paper it seems effortless, almost trite, to build an arrow between yourself and someone else. *Duh,* you just draw it in—and there it appears. Do some good leadership deeds, and *boom,* an arrow pops up. But this line of reasoning fails to recognize the significance of what is actually happening here.

First off, if you treat these arrows as disposable, hollow objects, then that is exactly what you will create. I love to cook. But some days, I'm just not really feeling it—not on my game—so I phone it in. I know what my paella is supposed to look like, but I'm just going through the motions. I skip steps. I cut corners. I make substitutions that will ultimately have a major impact on the end product. And when it's all said and done, my paella kind of sucks.

It looks like it's supposed to, and it tastes close enough,

but anyone who has had paella would know—something's off. And in all fairness, they'd be right. That paella wasn't up to par because I didn't give it the time and attention it needed. Maybe I was multitasking during dinner. Maybe I was just lazy and skipped a few details. Either way, it wasn't the paella I'm used to making. Leadership arrows, which are the result of relationships you're going to build with those on your team, are exactly like this. Except there's a lot more at stake here than just a mediocre dinner.

If you go out into this world with the singular goal of creating as many arrows as possible, as quickly as possible, you will find yourself oh-so-disappointed a year from now. Failing to give leadership the respect it deserves will leave you forever swimming upstream, in a constant and ultimately losing struggle to maintain ■ → ⊙ with those around you. Remember that game Hungry Hungry Hippos? The one where you set loose a tidal wave of miniature plastic balls in the middle of the board and gobble up as many as possible before your opponents? This isn't that.

Don't worry about quantity right now; in time, that will come. Quality should be at the front of your mind when it comes to establishing arrows. The goal being to create sturdy, pointy objects that are heavy as hell and can withstand the elements. Treat arrows like they're real, and you'll build meaningful and lasting arrows. Treating them like anything less isn't leadership—because those wouldn't be arrows.

※※※

The scariest thing about this theory of leadership is that it actually works, which is why I can't stress enough how important it is that you take the idea of building ■ → ⊙ seriously. This dynamic is human nature; do the correct things that result in someone choosing to follow you, and the arrow is built, period. The part I need to warn you about is that this works whether you have good intentions or not. I know you're here for the right reasons (to be a life-changing leader for everyone around you), but history has repeatedly shown us that this works—even for wretched, manipulative, evil human beings.

It almost always starts the same way. Someone with a platform to spread their message begins spewing some very simple—and vile—rhetoric: "Your Level 1 needs are at risk, and your family is not safe. And you know those people I dislike? They're the ones standing in your way." This is followed by some version of "And I'm the person that has a solution to get rid of them and make you safe and successful again. Just do what I say, hate who I hate, and you will be okay." They weaponize the psychological underpinnings of leadership, and hold our human needs and wants hostage in order to project their hateful agenda. The populace then feels obligated to elevate them to a position of power, at which point, this individual no longer needs influence to carry out their evil will, as they now possess the authority to make it into law. Although this has been done many times throughout history (and is still happening today), one of the most infamous individuals to do so was Adolf Hitler in 1930s Germany.

Hitler was a loser. He had no special skills, and he farted a lot (look it up). But he was a good orator in a time when this was critical to spreading one's message. Essentially, he was a convincing speaker and, it goes without saying, one of the most wretched human beings to have ever walked the planet. He had a very simple message: the plight of the German people was due to other races getting in the way, and it was primarily the fault of the Jews. To sum up years of hatred coming from his mouth, "In order for you [the German people] to be successful, you must first be safe, and the Jews are putting that at risk. I [Adolf Hitler] have a plan to take care of this and keep you and your family safe. Place me [Adolf Hitler] into a position of power, and I will take care of this." Evil in the truest sense. Sometimes you hear people ask the question, "If you had a time machine and could go back in time and kill baby Hitler, would you?" Easily, yes. Thrown into shark-infested waters without a second thought. But I digress.

Hitler manipulated the psychological foundation of why we, as humans, follow other humans. You can't force someone to follow you, but you can make it seem like not doing so would be a death sentence. And please don't think for one second that Adolf Hitler has been the only person in history to do this.

There are politicians today—all over the world but especially in the United States on both sides of the aisle—that use these same scare tactics to amass followers in hopes of rising to power. Although not to the extent of a genocidal dictator, these bureaucrats are weaponizing leadership to manipulate us into voting for them. Hoping that, by telling us our Level 1 needs are in doubt and diagnosing the culprits as those they disagree with, we will cave in through fear and vote for them. Have you ever seen a negative political ad on TV during an election year? "So-and-so voted for lighter sentences on violent crimes and wants to take away your rights . . ." My point exactly. It doesn't get more blatant than that.

History tells us that leadership is a powerful thing, and in the wrong hands, it can be downright deadly. Like I said earlier, I'm not here to critique your motivations for becoming a leader. Maybe you want to go into management one day and are preparing yourself for that next step. Maybe you just want to grow as a leader in the job you have now. Whatever your rationale, all I ask is this: please give the practice of leadership the respect it deserves. Building arrows with those on your team is, at its core, what leadership is. To be an effective leader, all you have to do is get someone to decide they want to you follow you. This happens when they need help with either their Level 1 or 2. Facilitating this because you care about them makes you a great leader—inserting your own agenda to manipulate them makes you something much, much less.

# Chapter 19
## The Connection

I'm making dinner. I lay out my crust, pour on the sauce, sprinkle on the cheese, then toss it in the oven. What emerges minutes later can only be described as heavenly—pizza—and all are happy. Now, let's pretend it's been an extremely long day full of pointless meetings. My mind is numb, and I find myself making dinner. I pour some sauce, place it in the oven, then add some cheese and a bit of dough. The result is a boiling hot soup, a far cry from my goal of pizza, and all are upset.

I need to use the restroom. I go in the bathroom, do my business, clean up, and wash my hands—success, and nobody is impressed. But the next time, for some unexplainable and troubling reason, I first do my business, then go into the bathroom, and finally wash my hands—tragedy, and all are deeply concerned. Whether we realize it or not, the order we do most things in life really (really, really) matters.

We can all relate to this. We perform a task that requires a series of steps, and somewhere along the way, we deviate from the plan and things go awry. And we usually don't realize just how important the order is until we screw it up. Building → between you and someone else (establishing a leadership dynamic) works the exact same way.

Every arrow you build will be uniquely its own, since it will be with uniquely different individuals. Leadership pizzas run the gamut on toppings and styles. Light sauce, extra pepperonis, half anchovies. However, every single one of those pies will start the same—with crust. Pizzas always, always, always start with crust, and leadership always starts with building a connection.

*\*\**

It's tempting, I know it is. To run outside your house, find the nearest person, and start being a leader. To grab them by the shoulders, shake them up a bit, and empower them to go out and be the best version of themselves—one they never dreamed was possible. In fact, while you're at it, you might as well just become a leader with everyone you come across today. See a random person, do some leadership, and *boom*, there's another arrow built. See ten thousand people, make ten thousand arrows. And although I would applaud you for having this mentality of wanting to sink your teeth in and go change the world, the only issue here is that, sadly, it won't work.

This is probably the most discouraging misstep for a new leader. They desperately want to do all the things we've discussed in this book, but when they go out and actually start doing them, the results are less than they were expecting. "I'm doing leadership stuff like you said, Joe. Why no arrows? I want a refund."

However, this frustration isn't reserved only for those new to leadership. It can also happen to established leaders when they join a completely new team (e.g., when taking a different job). Senior managers and executives commonly fall prey to this as well when leading large teams of people they've never met. And the diagnosis is always the same: a failure to establish a connection first. If you're going to have a meaningful effect on someone, there has to be a conduit for transferring, and ultimately receiving, actions from you to that person. In our physical world, this is a no-brainer. When it comes to leadership, it's a bit more unintuitive.

***

I'm going to call you. I dial my phone. That message gets sent through the air to the nearest cell tower, which then routes it along the cellular network, finding the closest cell tower to you, and then it's finally transmitted back through the air and to your phone. Now, imagine that for some bizarre and somewhat unsettling reason, you don't own a phone. Clearly, what I just described will not work. The analogy is absurdly simple, but if you don't have a cellular device to answer a call with, there is no way I can call you.

We're going tubing on the lake. I blow up the insanely dangerous inflatable raft that I will tug behind the boat at high speeds in hopes of jettisoning you off and into the water. We gas up the boat, throw on a bit of sunscreen, and we're on our way. At one point, I look back at you from across the lake and wonder, *Why isn't this working? Why are you so far away right now?* One of us forgot to attach the tow rope. I could drive around in circles all day, but unless we are connected, your experience will consist of sitting on the dock.

I'm a prankster and you're up next on my list. I've decided to douse you with water when you least expect it. I fill up my glass, head outside, and toss it in your direction. The only problem is that I live in Colorado, and you're at your house in California. The water falls harmlessly to the ground, and you remain safe and dry.

In every one of these scenarios, there is a physical limitation (literally physics) preventing you and me from interacting. No matter what one of us does, the other won't be impacted by it. You can dial random numbers all day long, but if the person you're trying to get a hold of doesn't have a cell phone—sorry, Charlie, that just won't work.

In real life, this is pretty easy to understand. If I am not physically connected to you either by proximity, technology, or some tangible connector—then you and I cannot impact one another. I could drive that boat up and down the lake until I run out of gas, but if you aren't with me on the water, nothing I do will be translated to you. It's the same with being a leader.

If you try to go out and help people with their Levels 1 and 2 but fail to establish a connection first, it won't go well. Don't get me wrong—people won't be mad at you for trying—you just won't be that effective, and you'll be confused and frustrated as to why. You'll spend a lot of energy with limited results. Perhaps one of the most common ways to see the importance of building a connection can be witnessed by going to the movies.

\*\*\*

It's freezing outside. Your nose is bright red and slightly runny from standing in line, but you don't care because this movie has been hyped up for years. *Avatar 9*—promised to be every bit as life changing as the first eight. You've seen the trailers, so you know it's an all-new blue cast, but that's fine with you. Eager to witness the 3D spectacle, you finally get inside the atrium, bypass the snack area since you've snuck in your own candy, and head into the theater. Awkwardly scootching your rear end past folks sitting near the aisle, you finally make it to your destination in the middle of the room. Tearing off your jacket, hat, gloves, and scarf—you are finally ready for the masterpiece that is *Avatar 9*.

The screen tells you to turn off your phone, the intro credits roll, and you're ready for things to start happening, fast. You want action. You want blue creatures zipping around the screen. You want two-plus hours of thrills and excitement. But what you get to start out with is something different. It's an opening scene, albeit brief, showing you a bit about the main character. Where she lives, her family, her love interest. It shows a side of her you wouldn't have known unless there was screen time strictly devoted to it. She projects empathy toward a loved one, she has a unique sense of humor, and above all else, she is just as normal of a "person" as you are, with feelings and emotions.

The director has peeled back the onion on our main heroine for a moment to reveal aspects of her that you can relate to, pieces of her that resonate in your life. In five minutes, they've built a quick connection between you and her. It isn't much. It won't last past the final credits, but it serves its purpose and is good enough for now.

Moments later, as she's being chased through the forest, you feel nervous for her, worried that she may not make it. You just saw that she's more than some random blue creature; she has a family, she has worries, she probably has a mortgage. You want her to be okay, and throughout the film, you feel actual emotions toward this completely made up, 100 percent not real character—which is the sign of a good movie. Not only do the filmmakers establish a connection with you, but they continue to build it throughout the film. Constantly reminding you this character demands your emotional investment and is someone you care enough about to sit through an entire movie for.

And it's because of these connections that some movie franchises just won't die. Even though the main actors in *Fast and Furious* will soon be parking their cars at the old folks' home, series like these are cash cows. We love the characters, and Hollywood knows that like an old concert T-shirt, we can't let them go. It's why there are fourteen *Spiderman* movies, and why on my deathbed I'll see a commercial for the seventh reboot of the *Ghostbusters*.

The inverse of this can be seen in how we start, and then quickly turn off, crappy Netflix movies all the time. Besides the fact that most of them simply aren't any good, I've realized what is happening. Usually, I just don't care. I'm not connected with the characters, so by twenty minutes in, it doesn't matter to me whether Samantha and John fall in love and get married, are sent to prison for tax evasion, or get eaten by giant spiders. That's not to say these films didn't try, but for whatever reason, the backstory or insights meant to resonate with me failed. Building a connection is the telltale sign of a good movie and should be considered, without a doubt, step number one in building an arrow (→) between you and someone else.

✳✳✳

Has a complete stranger ever tried to give you advice? To offer up their unsolicited opinion on some aspect of your life? Follow-up question: Did you care even one tiny bit what this complete rando had to say? Probably not. *Ew David, get away from me.* Unprompted commentary usually gets put where it belongs: in the trash. And it would go the exact same way if someone you didn't know walked up to you on the street and attempted to start encouraging, empowering, or inspiring you. "You can do it. I know you may have had a rough week, but it's all the past. You got this!" Sure, this might make you feel good in the moment, but it doesn't stick. Like tossing a gummy bear at a freight train—no effect. Trying to lead someone without first making a connection with them would result in the same outcome, even if you're not a stranger to the person.

Failing to make a meaningful connection before attempting to help a team member can come off as shallow, surface level, and almost fake to the one on the receiving end. Their thoughts can quickly skew to *I know they don't really mean it* or even *Am I being used for something?* In either case, without building a connection between you and someone you're trying to lead, just about all your efforts will be in vain.

It's for this exact reason that outsiders have such a difficult time gaining the trust of people on a team they are not a part of. We're inherently skeptical—wary—of people we think don't share our same goal. A great example of this is when you meet someone and learn they are from the same city or state as you. You both put down your armor for a second because you just found out that you are part of the same team, the "born and raised in Wisconsin" team. Deep-fried cheese, strong beer, and potential hypertension are all things you two share, and after discovering the bond between you, both of your demeanors are likely to change.

When your past leaders tried to encourage you, did it work? Did it actually have an impact? Of course it did. They had built a connection with you. When they dialed your cell phone number and sent it across the network, they were successful. You were able to pick up the phone and absorb the message—their actions had an actual impression on you. You knew they weren't trying to use you; it was genuine. They had already put in the work to establish and maintain a lasting connection with you. Without it, they'd just be speaking into the void.

And the most frustrating part is that you could be standing right next to someone, able to reach out and shake their hand, and they still won't be able to hear you unless this connection has been established. Thankfully though, it isn't that difficult to do. No magic involved. All you have to do to build a connection with someone is get them to have this thought:

"I know you care about me."

That's all it takes. Once you do that, the connection is built.

***

*I know you care* has a lot of weight to it. When you read it on paper, it seems trivial—just make someone realize you care about them. Simple, right? Getting to that point, to a place where another person honestly, truly, deep down in their core believes that you care about them as a human, is something completely different. It's the foundation to any lasting relationship, and ■ → ⊙ is no different.

If I don't think you care about me as a person—what I'm going through and my well-being—then everything you do in pursuit of leading me will be a waste of time. But if I know you are honestly trying to help me with my Levels 1 and 2 (that you're for real), then it becomes clear to me that you are someone worth following. You could also replace the word *connection* with *trust* since they are one and the same. I know you care = I trust you. Crucial because if for whatever reason I don't trust you, I won't leave my cocoon to follow you. I won't stray down the beach and attempt to start fishing like you do. I won't know if it's beneficial, or even safe. Without trust, without a connection, there can be no arrow.

\*\*\*

The topic of how to build trust with another human being is so nuanced and intertwined with our individual personalities and mannerisms that I'd be a fool to tell you, "Here is a step-by-step process for how to establish it with someone." I'd be setting you up for failure by offering that kind of advice.

To trust someone is to believe in them—their ability, strength, reliability, character, and so on. That's why I use "I know you care" synonymously with "I trust you." It's a little easier, more manageable, to describe how you get someone to realize you care about them. To get someone to say "I trust you" feels like it would require another eighty pages dedicated to the subject. More importantly though, I think phrasing it that way would give the illusion that there is a definitive way to go about establishing a connection. That there is some master blueprint hiding on the internet with a list of ways to build trust with someone. An overwhelming, forty-five-point plan that ends with someone saying "I trust you." Which is why, in my simple brain, it seems like a lot. Where would I even start? But if you told me, "Get that person to realize you care about them"—simple. I can do that. And so can you.

And yet, I'm not going to tell you how to care about another human being, because it would be weird if I had to do that. Supporting the well-being of other people is a requirement for becoming a leader, and this process could be very difficult for anyone not interested in or not capable of doing that. What I will do though is explain how we, as humans, often express that care, because once you recognize how we normally convey this to someone else, what appears as a giant cluster suddenly becomes much clearer. Which is why I'm proposing a full stop.

Halt.

Up to now, I've told you that leaders are people who help others with their needs and wants, but that we need to build a connection with someone before we're even able to do that. So, which is it? Are these separate tasks? Should I be scheduling three distinct meetings with people in order to effectively lead them? A three-course leadership meal with separate interactions built into the day? Thankfully, no.

As chaotic as it sounds, you actually end up doing all three with someone at once—building a connection while addressing L1 and L2. A leadership tossed salad, if you will. But we do this social multitasking every day of our lives, whether we are in the leadership role or not. It just seems tricky because you're after a specific goal in this instance: becoming an amazing leader. In reality, this behavior is commonplace for most people.

If you've ever gone out to dinner with friends, you have already experienced this sort of thing. And you weren't nervous, were you? To chew your food, swallow it, talk, drink your water, and laugh, all during the course of your meal? During that sixty-minute encounter, we seamlessly switch between these actions without even thinking. It happens naturally, and we are definitely not worried we're going to mess it up.

As a leader, but more so just as people in general, we interact with those around us in two very distinct ways. Once we're empowered with this knowledge, ascertaining the leader role becomes a lot less jumbled and a lot more tangible. But before we move on, let me be clear: establishing a connection opens the door for someone to follow you. It doesn't actually build the arrow.

You can't force someone to follow you; all you can do is pave the road for them. Without a connection, there is no path. There is no avenue allowing them to drive toward where you are or where you're going. It's just you doing things into the void of space, hoping that they stick. But once the lightbulb goes off in someone's head—"I know you care about me"—the connection has been made, and you're now able to lead them.

# Chapter 20
## A Leader's Actions

I wake up in a panic.

"How could this be? Have I failed for yet another year?" Jolting out of my sleeping bag, I look at the clock. It's 5:00 a.m. and reality is setting in. For the eighth year in a row, Santa Claus—that sneaky bastard—has eluded me. Lying awake on the floor of my parent's room, I reek with the stench of failure. I'm not sure what went wrong. I stayed awake for what felt like an eternity (in reality, only until 11:00 p.m.). As my grapefruit-sized brain starts devising next year's plan (forty mouse traps and a net), I start to fully realize that it's Christmas morning, the single greatest day in the entire year for a third grader. At this point, I'm certain of two things: there are gifts under the tree, and the smell of bacon seeping through the door means my grandpa is already awake.

Every morning, whether it was December 25, July 18, or any other random day in between, my grandpa would cook up bacon and eggs for breakfast. He was light-years away from what you'd call a healthy lifestyle, but he knew what he liked and stuck to his game, regardless of where he was. Which meant that for me, every Christmas morning started the same: crack open the door of my parent's room and immediately take a bacon-scented uppercut to the nostrils—forever entangling the scent of bacon with Christmas in my head.

Smells are unique that way. Just one whiff can instantly transport you back twenty years. One sniff of an old garage and I'm at my grandma's house, running around her backyard in my Power Rangers costume with my plastic sword. Fresh-cut grass sends me back to football practice in high school. And just last week, I smelled a candle that unfortunately opened a portal to ninth grade, with a scent nearly identical to an Abercrombie & Fitch cologne (please don't judge me, this is a safe space). Smells are a powerful thing. They can incite memories, instantly change your mood, and impact your entire day, especially if you happen across the wrong one. Emanating from one object, then traveling through the air and up into our noses—smells have a direct impact on our daily lives. Though the interesting thing about odor is that it can affect more than just the person smelling it. And as odd as it sounds, the best example of this comes from those tiny mischievous monsters we call children.

For little boys, for some strange and unexplainable reason, scents hold a mysterious, almost magical power. The worse the smell, the more intrigued their tiny minds are by it. Which naturally leads to a constant game of one-upmanship. As a former eight-year-old myself, as soon as you found a terrible odor—maybe it's a gym sock, maybe it's a stink bug, maybe it's something that emanated from you— you just had to share it. "Hey Jack, get a load of this," you say, shoving something putrid to his nostrils. And as it's being inhaled, you're able to instantly judge its pungency just by the look on his face. A furrowed brow equals success. If he starts to gag or looks physically disturbed by it, this certifies you really have got something special. You have directly impacted Jack with the smell you've shared. But it's important to recognize that anyone looking on, who sees Jack's face during all this, has been indirectly impacted by that scent as well.

"Don't smell what Joe has over there. It looked like Jack was going to pass out." Seeing the look on poor Jack's face tells anyone watching to stay clear of the odor in your possession. Although they didn't smell it themselves, they are now aware of it—indirectly—and have changed their day accordingly to avoid the same fate. It's akin to seeing someone walk past a dumpster in the summer and watching them cover their mouth to stop from dry heaving. If you were walking behind this person, you would know you need to change your course, else you too will be assaulted by the aroma of hot garbage. This is the indirect impact a scent can have, except it's usually far less overt.

Have you ever had a bad day and then randomly come across a scent you absolutely love? Fresh-baked cookies would fall into this category for me. Even at my worst, deep-in-a-funk kind of day, if I smell cookies hot out of the oven, I'm instantly put into a better mood. Not only does my own headspace change, but how I interact with the world does too. I'm happier, more patient, and slightly less of a pill to be around. It may be a small change, but my demeanor is different, and thus, how I interact with others is different as well. Anyone I come into contact with will be impacted—indirectly—by the scent of those chocolate-chip delights.

Put succinctly, our world stinks. Or perhaps more accurately, our world smells. And despite how hard we may try, we can never escape it. Scents run the gamut from good to disturbingly bad, and they can impact anyone that comes in contact with them. Whether we're the one directly experiencing the odor or we're indirectly feeling the consequences through watching someone else—our lives are constantly being altered by scent. The actions we take as leaders, but really, just as humans, are divided into similar categories. Understanding this division is crucial to leading another individual, and it's all but required to effectively lead teams of 100, 5,000, or 330,000,000 people.

\*\*\*

Take a moment and make a mental list of all the things you've done thus far today. Supermarket sushi? Bold choice, but it's okay because here we're only after the actions you took that impacted someone else. After all, we as leaders are out to help others, thereby becoming someone they want to follow. And as it pertains to supporting others, we instinctively zero in on the direct actions from our day. Those A to B—from ourselves (A) directly to someone else (B)—kinds of deeds. Holding the door open for someone at the store, telling a friend how much you appreciate them, piggybacking the elderly across the street. Actions that had a direct impact on someone else in that moment.

Direct actions are pretty straightforward in that way, which is why they jump off the page at us. Sometimes it's a physical action, like helping a friend move; sometimes it's monetary, like giving someone a gift; and other times it can be verbal, as in offering words of encouragement. In every case, we performed a deed that directly impacted someone else. Helping lift a couch with B, handing B a present, telling B everything is going to be okay. Our days are jam-packed with these direct actions, and they're pretty easy to spot. We (A) spend time doing an action that is immediately received by someone else (B). B cuts A off in traffic—A gives B the bird. A to B. Doesn't get more straightforward than that.

However, direct actions can also take on a slightly different, far less obvious form. The type of deed that was perhaps overlooked when you made your list. Have you ever said something in hopes of getting a laugh? Ever share a vulnerable fact about yourself to put a friend at ease? Utter the words *I'm so sorry* as someone shares a sad story from their life with you? These are all direct actions too. They're tiny and often go unregistered in our heads. They come and go in a flash, so as you reflected on your day, I wouldn't be surprised if you glossed over them. Most of us don't realize just how often we are directly impacting others.

- A asks B how they're doing and expresses empathy toward B's situation.

- A smiles and waves at B as they walk by in the hallway.
- A shares a funny story to lighten the mood in a meeting with B.

The definition of a direct action is anything done that directly impacts someone else, and they are usually what comes to mind when we think of leadership: empowering, inspiring, motivating—and you wouldn't be wrong. This is by far the most straightforward way to build a connection and support someone. And at this point, I wouldn't blame you for demanding, "Okay Joe, just give me the damn list already. The secret sauce of which actions I should be doing for which application." Well, I hate to disappoint, but there isn't a special set of connection-building actions, a separate pile for L1, and then a third group for Level 2.

In fact, hardly any of the actions we take are absolutes.

For example, snapping your fingers can be done to keep rhythm with a song, indicate that you'd like things sped up, or in a sassy manner across your face. One action—creating noise by quickly rubbing two fingers together—used in three very different manners. Whistling can be done to create "music" and annoy everyone around you, call for your dog, or express approval at a sporting event. Saying hello to someone can be used as a greeting, in a sarcastic manner, or in traffic when another vehicle isn't behaving how you'd like ("Um, *hello*?!"). It's incredibly rare to find an action that serves only one purpose, an absolute action. Leadership is no different.

The classics: inspire, empower, encourage, engage, challenge, motivate. The tried-and-true actions of a leader, and all 100 percent relative. It's how you leverage these actions, not specifically what they are, that determines how they're received. You can encourage Laura to take the next step in her career (L2), but you can also encourage her not to feel ashamed about taking a mental health day after she tells you news from her personal life. You can challenge Bill to enroll in a professional certificate course outside of work because you believe in his potential (L2), but you can also challenge him to take a vacation and spend some needed time away from the office (L1). In each case, you are impacting someone via your actions, but your intent—and thus how it is being consumed—is very different. Once I realized this nuance—that leadership actions are relative and not carved in stone—the idea of becoming a leader got much simpler (and a lot less overwhelming) in my head.

Nothing about leadership is absolute, which includes the actions we take. Great leaders recognize that those gold-standard leadership deeds are simply vessels, mechanisms at our disposal to impact those around us. They can be used toward building a connection, helping with basic needs, or supporting the success of a team member. Your intent (how you manifest and employ that action) changes how it will be absorbed and metabolized. Below are some ways that I, Joe Reichert, have done this with others. I can't stress this enough—this is my list of what has worked for me in the past. This is not a comprehensive set, nor is it direct guidance for you. And I'm definitely not saying, "Though shall go out and do these things." I understand it's nice to have examples, so I'm going to cautiously list some, but promise me you won't take this as law. Just something to get the juices flowing.

\*\*\*

I'm an introverted extrovert. I love being around people and conversing, but I recharge my batteries by being at home with my wife and our lump of a dog. Social encounters don't give me anxiety, but I'd much rather keep things light by cracking a joke to put everyone (mostly myself) at ease. As a result, how I interact with others and the direct actions I take often mirror my personality (and yours do too).

When it comes to making a connection with those around me, humor, vulnerability, and empathy are my "power three." Laughing is universal. We may not find the same things funny, but whether you're a 2-year-old in diapers or a 102-year-old in diapers, we all laugh. Sharing a moment like this with someone immediately lowers their guard, even if for a moment, so they can feel comfortable around me.

And in the attempt, I usually end up sharing something vulnerable about myself that is humorous, thereby opening my armor to reveal that I too am just a normal, quirky, flawed person. Something we clearly have in common.

And finally, I use empathy nonstop when I speak with other people. Not every conversation is silly and light-hearted (nor should it be). There are times when some very real topics come up. When this happens, my entire goal is for the other person to feel safe in sharing whatever they'd like with me. Although I don't explicitly say it, I try to make it known that their life isn't a bother to me. Hearing about it doesn't inconvenience me. In fact, it's quite the opposite: I actually do care about what they're going through. They're a member of the team and I want what's best for them. By actively listening, matching tone, and offering words of condolence or encouragement, I'm able to prove to them that I'm someone who cares. I'm not just going through the motions and patiently waiting for them to finish speaking. Not everyone uses humor, and sometimes being vulnerable is scary, but empathy is something we can all do, and I would recommend leveraging it every chance you get.

At work, this is most easily done by asking someone how they're doing. Warning: they will likely reply with a courteous and surface-level "I'm good, how are you?" At which point, you need to either follow up with a specific question to get the conversation going ("So, how was your hike up Mt. Bierstadt last weekend?") or borrow a move from my own playbook and reply with "No-no-no, how are you *really* doing?" then go silent. This has become my go-to as I connect, or reconnect, with people on my teams. Simply asking how someone is doing has turned into a formality these days. I have a boss who asks me this. I say fine, and then we move directly into work topics. There is in no way, shape, or form a connection between us (they've made it abundantly clear they don't care). By making it known that you really want to hear how someone is doing, you are broadcasting to them in neon letters, "Just so you are aware, I actually do care about you," and this usually results in a connection-worthy conversation.

As far as helping people with their Levels 1 and 2, my approach comes in all shapes and sizes. The connection-building portion of a conversation usually ends up highlighting a path for me to assist them with their basic human needs. At work, L1 is all about our "real life"— grandma is in the hospital, these are the daycare pickup times, etc. Once I know what is going on in someone's life, I'm then able to find the most appropriate way to provide support. As a manager, I've found that making work flexible when it needs to be and accommodating people's schedules are among the most impactful ways to do this. Nothing is more stressful than trying to be in two places at once (as it's technically impossible), so I always advise against it. If you have to take a sick kid to the doctor, help a relative, or do anything else that requires undivided attention, by all means, do it. Even if your occupation doesn't allow for such a flexible work schedule, you can always find small ways to make that person's work–life balance more manageable. You'd be shocked how far the little things go in helping someone with their Level 1 needs.

As far as Level 2 is concerned, there is nobody that believes in a teammate's potential more than I do. I have no problem telling someone how great I think they can be, even if they themselves don't see it yet. This usually comes out as a direct action via words of encouragement, as well as other deeds intended to empower and challenge someone to be their most successful self. As a manager, nothing says "I know you're ready for your next step" like giving someone an increase in responsibility (and then recognizing them for it). But you don't need to be in a position of authority to help someone with L2. Words are free, and a little encouragement or recognition from a peer can go a long way.

In my day-to-day life, I'm constantly leveraging direct actions to be a better leader for those on my teams. As you've seen and can probably attest to, direct actions take on a variety of forms, and they can be performed—and thus consumed by others—in an infinite number of ways. But thinking that direct actions (the things we do from A to B) are the only actions leaders take would be like taking a nosedive through a trapdoor. There are two kinds of actions that leaders must be versed in. Failing to realize the second type means forever falling into the pit of mediocre leadership.

# Chapter 21
## The Wild West

Welcome to the Wild West of leadership. Deep space, the bottom of the ocean, giant black holes—indirect actions are without question the most overlooked and misunderstood aspect of leadership. They're unsolved mysteries that are almost entirely unexplored, with 99.995 percent of us having no idea they exist, and the other 0.005 percent unable to put them into words. Indirect actions are what allow us to lead people we've never met, and ironically, they are the easiest way to make a large impact on any team you're a part of. Yet we fail to recognize them, so they continue to fly under the radar, always there, lurking in the shadows whether we realize it or not. But let me assure you, they aren't scary, they're not complicated, and they don't bite. Watch how simple this is.

Amy holds the door open for Dan (A to B). Liz (C) witnesses this happen and is motivated to hold the door open for someone else who walks in. Two sentences were all it took. Amy to Liz (A >> C). Watch, I'll do it again.

Adam encourages Ryan not to quit on his New Year's resolutions. Chris hears this interaction and is encouraged to persevere on his goals as well. Adam to Chris. Again.

Alex attempts to cheer up Paul. Paul is then in a better mood when speaking to Carey. Alex to Carey. I could go all day.

Indirect actions are just things we do that indirectly impact someone else. They come in a host of flavors, with the examples above being direct actions (A to B) that were eventually consumed by a third party (C).

$$(A \text{ to } B) \gg C$$
where $\gg$ is physical, visual, or auditory

In one case, this happened visually when Liz saw Amy perform a direct action for Dan, which in turn sparked something in her brain motivating her to do the same. In another, it was through a sort of action-osmosis: Carey interacted with Paul, who was in a better mood after speaking with Alex. These are the most prominent type of indirect action: direct actions that are felt by those who were not the intended target. Once you realize what they are and just how often they're occurring, it's amazing (and slightly terrifying) to think about how large of a wake we produce on a daily basis. Take the benign example of holding a door open for someone.

A holds the door open for B. C sees this and decides they too will hold the door, this time for D and E. F spots this interaction as they approach and decides to hold the door for G. H is leaving the building and walks through the door that F is holding for G and says, "Thank you I appreciate it," to F. J hears this while walking by and has the urge to call her mom and tell her how much she appreciates her. It's a clichéd, Hallmark-card type of scenario, one that could be the opening scene of a '90s rom-com, but it's true: our actions cause ripples. Great leaders recognize this and use it to their advantage.

Where I currently work, this is still a mystery to most. Our executives waste millions of dollars every year in failed leadership initiatives due to their inability to recognize the impact indirect actions can have. Don't be dumb like most executives. Use indirect actions to become a better and more effective leader. When done correctly, they allow us to achieve something truly remarkable: leading people we've never met.

***

Earlier in the book, I asked you to list a few people that you consider great leaders. If you named a president or a high-profile, famous individual, odds are you have never come in contact with this person. And yet, you still consider them leaders. You're choosing to follow this individual even though you've never had a direct interaction with them (a face-to-face conversation, email exchange, phone call, etc.). This person is doing things that are having enough of an impact on your life—indirectly—that you've decided they are worthy of following. Actions that you saw, heard, or felt—potentially from thousands of miles away. You absolutely consider them to be a great leader, and yet you've never met them.

Somehow, they were able to connect with you and then prove themselves as someone who wants to help you with your basic needs and wants, thereby becoming a leader in your mind. The only way this happens is through indirect actions. And here's the kicker: indirect actions can not only be felt miles away, but also decades later. As in, they allow you to continue leading people even after you're dead.

Abraham Lincoln will forever make my list of the greatest leaders (as evidenced by how often I reference him in this book). He died in 1865, so clearly there have been zero direct actions between Abe and myself. Yet when I read books about him, I feel connected to the man: his personality, his mannerisms, his sense of humor, his vulnerabilities and deep insecurities. His actions while president—taking the first steps toward racial equality in the United States and not backing down in the face of a civil war—are still impacting American citizens today, and he's been dead for over 150 years. Indirect actions are incredible that way. But you don't have to be a president to make them work for you.

Regular folks (you and I) can use indirect actions just as much as any statue-worthy leader can. And no—you don't need social media, a prestigious career, or a large online presence to do it. Start small. You'd be shocked just how far your impact can travel as someone first starting out. Here are a few examples of how this can be done today, right now.

- Stand up for someone in a conversation who isn't there to defend themselves. Other people see this courage and are empowered to do the same in the future.
- Recognize someone for the work they've done on your team and tell them how much you appreciate them. You'll make their week, meaning anyone else they encounter will be positively impacted, and others will likely follow suit and be moved to express gratitude within the team.
- Go out of your way to help a teammate with an assignment. Others will see this team-first example and follow suit in supporting their peers.

All of these cause indirect actions to reverberate throughout your team. Sometimes the shockwaves happen quickly, and other times it's a slow burn. Either way, when it comes to having a large impact on your team, indirect actions are far and away the easiest method. As a newcomer, a good rule of thumb is to try to directly impact those around you and let your actions saturate throughout the team. Do so many positive things for other people that the impact you're having is unmistakable. Trust me, people will notice. You may think to yourself, "I'm too far down the food chain; nobody will be impacted by what I do. It will never be seen or heard about," and you'd be absolutely wrong. Even the smallest actions, when absorbed or felt by the right person, can have a huge impact. And never forget that once we have a connection with someone, our actions are always being felt by them—whether we intended it or not.

***

Throw a rock into a pond and you get a splash (science), followed immediately by ripples emanating from the point of impact. Tadpoles, baby ducks, and dragonflies all start bobbing up and down as the waves roll by. And whether you threw that rock into the water on purpose or it accidentally dropped out of your sweaty little fingers, it's going to cause ripples. One action, rock hitting water—regardless of how or why it got there—impacts every life on that tiny pond. I said that indirect actions can be almost magical, but I should've also mentioned that they're always there. And once you've made a connection with someone, you're always indirectly impacting them.

Every action you take that is seen, heard, or shared by someone else, no matter your intention, will turn into an indirect action for them. Speak poorly about someone behind their back, bend the rules when you think no one is looking, skip steps because nobody will care—a club of "victimless crimes"—all of these create toxic ripples on the pond. As leaders, it's crucial to remember we're always on. When someone sees, hears, or feels an action you've taken, it doesn't matter whether you said "It's all good, I'm just acting as Joe-schmo right now" or "Okay, now I'm acting in my official leader role"—your behavior is turning into indirect actions and impacting your team.

Once you've earned the leader role, everything you do is being done by a leader. You don't get to ask people to momentarily think of you as just another team member. Just another Larry in accounting who quietly keeps to himself, and on occasion does and says some semi-unprofessional stuff. Doesn't work that way. You've earned the leader role, and now it's yours—all the time. Like it or not, all day long, you're tossing rocks into your team's pond. And all day long, those around you are bobbing up and down on their lily pads as a result of your actions.

It can take a long time to earn the leader role from some individuals on your team. I've experienced situations after starting a new job where it's taken me months to accomplish this. To build meaningful connections with people who have been spited or used in the past by previous bosses can be a difficult endeavor. I had to constantly prove to them, "I actually care about you, this isn't for show," and eventually, after many months, I was able to get them to trust me, and I started having an impact on them. And after all that—the countless hours of establishing a connection and helping others with their Levels 1 and 2—one wrong indirect action can erase it all.

There are no off days when you're a leader. And if you're thinking to yourself that being an incredible leader takes a lot of work, you're right.

# Chapter 22
## It Takes Work

1. I'll have the burger please, but instead of fries, can I do a bunch of pickles on the side?
2. Can I please get the fish and chips, but can you have them fry everything twice and also swap the vinegar for five more tartar sauces?
3. I'll do the cobb salad with extra bacon, avocado, and egg. And can you hold half of the lettuce? I think I'm in a toppings kind of mood, thank you.

All equally ridiculous, and all actual orders I have placed in the past. My wife says I'm too picky, and yet she's a gorgeous doctor that I met when I was twenty-nine years old—so you tell me how that's working out. Yes, I will wait for a booth. And no, I'm not sitting by the server station. Going out to eat is an experience and should be treated as one, because restaurants really are a thing of beauty.

Hungry, we shlub ourselves in the door, are handed a menu or told to scan a tiny square, and then proceed to request items that are either altered—or sometimes completely absent—from the menu. We might spend twenty minutes scouring the options, trying in vain to find something we'd like to eat, with the server having all but forgotten about us. Then, all of a sudden, something hits us and we've magically reached menu nirvana. For whatever unknown reason, we now know exactly what we want to eat, and bless our souls, it might not reside on the menu. At least not how it's being presented to us. So we flag down our server and list off our desired sustenance. We know what we want—this detailed and customized entrée in all its personalized glory—specifically made for us.

Often, if the request is within reason, the kitchen says they'll do it. If it's off the wall, they may say "Get bent, we're not making that." And other times, they might respond with "We can do XYZ, will that do instead?" It's hit or miss what kind of chef you'll run into. The better the establishment, the more likely you are to get accommodated.

Now, I'd like you to meet Jeff.

Jeff is a chef and has wanted to be one his whole life. Jeff went to culinary school, has multiple Ginsu knives, and has watched hundreds of hours of *Diners, Drive-ins, and Dives*. He understands food, the science behind it, and how to create wonderful works of editable Instagram art. Unfortunately, at this point in Jeff's career, he has decided to only serve meatloaf. Order a salad, receive a meatloaf. Ask for a burger, get some more meatloaf. Loaves and loaves for days. Regardless of what you're in the mood for, Jeff is serving up meatloaf. One star on Yelp.

And honestly, that makes sense. Jeff sucks. He's nice, but he doesn't get it. If you saw on LinkedIn that Jeff got fired, you'd go "Yep, that sounds about right. Jeff clearly doesn't grasp the concept of being a chef." When asked later about his termination, Jeff is confused. "What do you mean I have to make food for each individual person? That sounds like a lot of work." Yes Jeff, yes it is. But great chefs, just like great leaders, understand that customizing their approach for each person is all part of the job.

Whenever I speak with new leaders, I always make it a point to tell them that being a leader is extremely rewarding and I love being one, but it's rarely a glamorous role. As you've seen, it takes a good bit of work to get someone else to want to follow you. Constantly doing the right things and putting their needs and wants before your own can sometimes drag on a person. That's why the path to mediocre leadership is paved with good intentions.

Leadership is not a passive activity. Recognizing what needs to be done isn't enough. Reading this book is a great start, but telepathy isn't real, and you can't will support onto someone. So to all the wishful thinkers out there, I love you—but you're not leaders. You actually have to go out and earn the leader role with everyone on your team, all the time. It requires action. Getting off your ass, even when you don't want to, and helping those on your team. And be forewarned: there will absolutely be days where you wake up and aren't feeling it.

It would be a disservice to let you believe that leaders are these super humans who never get worn out or tired of putting others first. Who never want to skip a day, stay in bed, and let others figure it out. Truthfully, I feel this way more often than I'd care to admit. After all, you're giving pieces of yourself away to others all day long—which can be extremely draining, and it's exactly why leadership is so often compared to parenting.

\*\*\*

Most books dance around the idea of leadership. They list off the traits, tendencies, and characteristics of great leaders but rarely dissect what leadership actually is. And one of the most common comparisons to describe leadership is with parenting. Which I absolutely agree with, as I feel this way toward my own teams.

First off, parents (good parents, at least) always want what's best for their children. They instinctively do things to guarantee their offspring's survival, but they also want them to be happy and live successful lives. A large part of a parent's life is ensuring their children's L1 and L2 are being met, much like a leader does for those on their team. And often, parents will put the needs and wants of their kids before their own, also much like a great leader. So don't

158 | Leader Relativity

be alarmed if, down the road, you feel an almost maternal or paternal bond toward those on your team. It's not disrespectful (please don't actually treat them like children). You're just experiencing the effects of what *I actually care about you* does to a person. However, you may only have three children, but you can have five hundred people on your team that you need to lead and do this for.

***

It's the holiday season as I write this, and I can't help but think how much I love and hate snow. We have a unique relationship, snow and I. Beautiful to look at, agonizing to shovel. Providing ambience when viewed out our living room window, and hazardous when seen through a car windshield. We call our dog Polly "snowflake" because she is so dainty and high maintenance. But snowflakes (as clichéd as it sounds) are a great metaphor to describe people—every snowflake is different, just like all people. And I don't just mean looks; I mean deep down in our basic operating systems. Personalities, mannerisms, preferences, fears, triggers—there will never be two people that are identical—which makes it that much more difficult to establish ■ → ⊙ with those around you.

You may be thinking to yourself, "Duh"—and yes, I agree with you. But because every ■ is different, with their own unique set of needs and wants, it means that every → will also be different. There is no "rinse and repeat" blueprint for earning the leader role. No list of actions and conversations that under every circumstance will take you to your end goal of ■ → ⊙. It's on you to figure this out. Sure, sometimes you'll have some very expressive and communicative people on your team that broadcast their L1 and L2 for you, but in my experience, this is very rare. Usually, I have to go out of my way to get to know people, learn about their lives, and then find ways to serve them. That's really what I mean when I say leadership takes a lot of work. Not only are you out there building connections and helping people, but you must make an effort to first uncover what those needs and wants are, and then understand each individual enough to interact with them in a meaningful way.

I work a lot with engineers. As a whole, I think they're given a bad rap, but when it comes to preconceived ideas on how they interact with the outside world, sometimes the shoe does fit. I've run into absolutely brilliant minds, ones that are on their way to changing the world from a technology they will one day invent, but long-winded, cheery chats about last weekend are not a priority for them. As such, I don't try to trap them in those types of conversations. I want them to be comfortable, and it's not their job to match my personality. As difficult as it is to change my style and cadence, in order to have any chance of making a connection with them, I must alter how I communicate so it is effective for them (often, this means short bursts of dialogue, just up to the point that they are okay with, and then I disengage). And let me tell you, doing this for fifty people can take a toll—but you can't quit.

***

Jay-Z has one of my favorite lines in all of hip-hop: "What you eat don't make me sh*t." It's a little aggressive for what I'm trying to convey, but it is absolutely appropriate when it comes to your actions as a leader.

My good friend Jay and I walk into a restaurant, and we're starving. It's been a day of nonstop cartwheels, dance-offs, and driving around in exotic cars. We sit down and order our food. I'm having fish and chips, and Jay is having something fancy (which is fine, he's paying). After ten minutes, my food comes out, but the staff alerts us that the posh nature of Jay's dish means it won't be ready for another half hour. Jay, being a considerate mogul, tells me to go ahead and start eating. I, famished from the events of our day, consume my meal in what feels like seconds. I finish my last bite, stuffed to the gills, and put my napkin on my plate. I look over at Jay—and you're never going to believe this—but he's still hungry.

Imagine that. Seeing someone eat doesn't make you full. It's a no-brainer because eating is the quintessential nontransferable act; I eat, and you stay hungry. Building arrows (→) with those on your team is the same way.

You may spend hours and hours earning the leader role from someone on your team. Painstakingly figuring out how best to support them in their quest to survive and succeed in this world. Understanding what makes them tick and how best to connect with them. And I'm here to tell you—great job. That is what leadership is all about. However, that arrow you just spent so much time building is absolutely nontransferable to someone else.

Sure, sometimes the actions you take are consumed indirectly by others, and you can build your arrows that way (many at a time). But when that isn't happening, and your direct actions are being received only by their intended target, then there is no arrow building going on with anyone else.

Cooking for Sara doesn't feed Kim. Actions done for Nate in a vacuum don't help Tyler. These arrows you're building, the things that define you as a leader, are nontransferable and, as such, must be individually built with every person on your team. So just because Erin considers me a leader because I've earned that with Erin doesn't mean Jack will, or Ben, or Mia. You have to go out and actively build arrows with every person on your team. I wasn't kidding—being a great leader is a lot of work.

And here's the kicker. Those arrows you just built from the ground up, through hours of personalized leadership (the only kind of leadership)—every single one of them can disappear if not cared for properly.

# Chapter 23
## High Frequency

I have a very special set of skills that not many possess. If given responsibility of a plant, flower, or interior shrub, I can have it dead within one week under my supervision. A sort of gardening hit put on it with almost no chance of escape. Just seven days is all it takes for me to have that thing looking like an old banana. I don't mean to, but for some reason, when it comes to horticulture, I'm like Charles Barkley swinging a golf club—not pretty.

And it's not for lack of trying. When I remember the plant exists, I'm all over it. Watering, pruning, and whatever else plants require. But for some reason, it just always slips my mind. I could walk past a plant five thousand times and not have it speak to me (*Hey man, you should really water me*). Not a word. Then, a week later, my wife will ask me why Stevie (we name our plants) has passed away. The only response I can give is "Whoops," and hope that Stevie is in a better place.

Plants are funny like that: don't water them and they die. Finicky buggers. But probably the most frustrating part is that you can be on the top of your game for years, watering a plant religiously, then all of a sudden go on vacation for a couple weeks and come back to a wilting mess. No water and no sunlight equals a direct path to mummified brown garbage. No matter how long you've been caring for that plant, if all of a sudden you stop giving it what it needs to survive, then that's all she wrote. ■ → ⊙ is the same way. Not acting like a leader to someone on your team means the arrow between you two will dry up, fade away, and eventually disappear.

I told you earlier to picture the arrows you're building as real, tangible objects. The kind you can run into if you're not paying attention. Though I left out one important thing: you really have to treat each arrow as a living, breathing organism to be a successful leader. Something that requires your attention on a regular basis. You have to bring it water, clip the branches, and ensure it is growing correctly. Being a good leader means doing actions that serve others, thereby making them more productive members of your team. And you must do these things all the time—with high frequency.

That's the epitome of what a role is. You can leave a functional duty dormant for a long time, and when you come back it will still be there, right as you left it, largely unchanged. Roles aren't like that. Yes, they're given out by others on your team, but they're constantly being re-given, meaning they must constantly be re-earned. If I, as a member of your team, see you as someone that can help me with my Levels 1 and 2, then I'll choose to follow you. But every day, I have new needs and new things I want to accomplish. So every day, I'm subconsciously looking for someone to help me with them. And if you've had a history of doing this for me in the past, then I'll give you a bit of leeway in doing it again, but eventually I have to do what's best for me. It's not personal, and I likely won't even realize I'm doing it, but I will find someone else to follow if it comes to that. The arrows you're building should be treated as living, breathing organisms. Neglect them, and they will disappear.

*⁎*

I need to clarify something before we move on. I told you earlier that it's possible, through indirect actions, for people to consider you a leader long after you're dead—which is probably confusing at this moment. Here's what's happening.

Take Martin Luther King Jr. as an example. The embodiment of leadership, and someone most of us continue to regard as a leader to this day. That's because Dr. King's actions while he was alive are still indirectly impacting most of us on a daily basis. They were so large, so monumental, so documented, that they live on long after his death. The greater the impact you have on someone, the longer you can go without watering the arrow. But let me be very real for a minute: you and I are not at the level of an MLK right now. Our actions, though impactful, do not resonate in our pond the same way his did, and still do. That's not to say we can't get there, but at this moment, both of us are producing waves that are much, much smaller.

If we don't toss another rock into the water (do an action to help someone either directly or indirectly), our ponds will eventually go still. Dr. King's actions produced a wake so large they will forever reverberate around that pond, continuing to create ripples and impact others for decades to come. He continues to influence us simply by our seeing, hearing, or learning about the actions he took.

So, in this instance, the arrow between myself and Dr. King is still being watered and cared for. He's no longer doing new actions, but the ones he did while alive are still making their way to me—indirectly—thereby making him someone I choose to follow. So I still consider Dr. King to be a great leader, even though he passed long ago.

It is absolutely possible to get to that point one day, but it doesn't happen overnight. And a word of caution: the desire to have that large of an impact on society is dangerously close to the desire to be famous, which is not at all important to great leaders. Helping people is one thing. Being publicly recognized for it is another. Do the right things for long enough, and people will choose to follow you. Your actions will start creating a larger and larger wake, and you will eventually amass a large following. But this occurs on an individual basis, and it doesn't happen overnight. There are no shortcuts to becoming a leader. Be patient and stay the course. It is possible that over time, your actions, like Dr. King's, will start to live on and impact others even when you're not present to see it happen. Just remember that for a leader, fame and effectiveness are not linked.

***

I read a leadership book once that had me rate myself as a leader. If I had to guess, I think at that time I probably gave myself a 5 out of 10. I wasn't in a position of functional authority yet, nor was I quite sure what leadership actually was. I just knew that I hadn't really done much of it, so I figured 5 out of 10 was a safe place to land. Looking back on it, reading that book was probably one of the dumbest and most confusing things I could've done, and without a doubt, it royally screwed up my interpretation of what it means to be a leader.

I understand what the author was trying to do. If you know where you stand today, it's possible to measure your progress down the road, thereby giving you some tangible number to quantify success. Seeing a positive change makes you feel good: "It's working!" However, what that author (and so many others since) failed to realize was that leadership ($\blacksquare \rightarrow \odot$) happens on an individual basis and is therefore relative. This dynamic doesn't transfer from person to person, and most importantly, it isn't static. To say you're an 8 as a leader would be like proclaiming, "I'm a best friend." Okay great, but with who? Everyone? Just Amanda and Claire? It makes no sense. But if you're determined to give yourself a leadership score, then we have to recognize that effectiveness as a leader—your "score"—is unique to each follower.

Let's say you consider yourself a great leader and that before reading this book, you would've self-scored at a 9. Now, pretend for a moment that you're invited to a holiday party for your significant other's work. You get all dressed up: dress, heels, the whole enchilada. Park the car, walk in the cold for two blocks, and make your way into the restaurant—but once you get inside, you don't recognize a soul. It's a company you don't work for, comprised of people you have never met. One hundred complete strangers making small talk and getting buzzed on free mulled wine. You know how many people in this room, at this exact moment, consider you a leader? Zero. You know that leadership score of a 9 that you gave yourself earlier? It's actually a zero with every person in this room. There is not one arrow established between you and anyone on this team. For starters, you're not even a part of this team (your significant other is), which makes it impossible for you to have already built a leadership dynamic with anyone there. Now, in the time you will spend together at this party, you are all on a transient team that will disperse at the end of the night, but it is only during this brief time that you could begin to become a leader (if for some reason that was your goal).

It's the same reason that when you walk down the street and pass a stranger, they have no idea if you're a leader. You've never met. There is no ■ → ⊙ dynamic between the two of you. Your leadership score with that person would be a zero, since your frequency of interacting with them is nonexistent. Our effectiveness as leaders is relative to each person on our team. You can spend a lot of time impacting a few individuals and be an 8 with them. However, there could be others that you have neglected or not supported in a while, and you'll only be a 3 with them. And get this, you can be an 8 with someone today, but in a month be at a 5. Our effectiveness as a leader (our leadership score) happens at the individual level and is not static. Without continuous watering, arrows will wilt, deteriorate, and eventually die.

And here's the best part of all—we don't even get to pick our own score. Followers determine that, not the other way around. They're the ones choosing to give us the leader role. If that desire is strong, you could say we have a high score. But if that desire wanes and they no longer want to go where we go (because their Levels 1 and 2 aren't being met), then our score decreases.

So technically, you can't even score yourself in leadership—it's not yours to give out. You'd have to ask everyone on your team to rate you, and then you'd need to refer to all those scores individually to assess how you're doing.

And on the off chance you did do that, you'd find a striking correlation: your scores are directly proportional to the amount of time spent supporting that individual. In other words, the frequency of how often you're performing as a leader is directly correlated to the score a follower would give you. Water plants and they grow. Go away for long enough, neglecting their wants and needs, and the arrow wilts. You can't be a leader to someone once a month or once a week. To be a great leader, you have to be one, acting like one, all the time.

In the beginning, this is going to take a conscious effort on your part. Though there will come a day when being a leader is woven into your DNA—and that's what we're after.

# Chapter 24
## Going Critical

When I first grew my mustache, someone at work told me I looked like a GI Joe from the 1980s. It came from another man, so I took it as a compliment (the way I think he meant it), but the encounter does highlight our inability to effectively communicate amongst the male gender. I also received *Civil War train conductor, old-timey barber,* and *guy who gets shot out of a cannon.* Slightly odd and well-meaning commentary toward the soup strainer I now had on my upper lip. Though my favorite bit of feedback was probably *extra in a sci-fi thriller.* I still have my mustache, meaning a cameo is still in the cards for me. And when it comes to science fiction and evil geniuses, there is nothing more terrifying than when the nuclear reactor you are using *goes critical.*

Immediately, hazard lights start flashing and sirens wail, indicating there is something extremely dangerous afoot. I picture an old, disheveled scientist with hair like they're constantly being electrocuted (i.e., Albert Einstein), standing next to a control panel mashing away at the controls. Bright red buttons, yellow dials, and levers that say "EMERGENCY" in bold, all being pressed and pulled in an attempt to control the chaos. We all know what happened at Chernobyl and, to a lesser extent, Three Mile Island; nuclear reactors are formidable systems that command our respect. Characters in movies use them for powering giant lasers and sending spaceships into the next galaxy, while those of us in the real world usually rely on them for breakfast waffles, drying our hair, and setting the mood—in other words, electricity.

Yet, for how much we use and rely on nuclear power, we're blissfully unaware of how it works, leading to some major misconceptions. "Going critical" has become synonymous with a dangerous nuclear meltdown, when in reality it is one of the most important steps in the operation of a reactor. Nuclear fission is when the nucleus of an atom splits into smaller parts and, in doing so, creates energy. When this happens, neutrons are ejected from the atom and sent outward, looking for a new home. That newly single neutron is quickly absorbed by a neighboring atom, causing that nucleus to become unstable and thus break apart—in the process creating energy and more newly single neutrons. Over and over again this happens. Atoms split, create energy, and expel neutrons. Those get absorbed by a new atom, which splits, creates energy, and expels more neutrons. The point where this process becomes self-sustaining is referred to as going critical. It's the desired outcome for any nuclear reactor, and it's what all leaders are ultimately striving for.

It's for this reason I'd like you to say goodbye to who you are today. I'm sure that person's great and that the two of you have had quite a ride up to this point, but things are about to change. In the beginning, you won't notice much. In fact, leadership might seem like a chore to you at times. You'll see this book on your shelf and think, "How have I helped someone, led someone, today?" You'll stand up from your desk, venture out into the office, and start supporting others. At that point, it isn't second nature yet, and you haven't quite formed the habit, but you're still out there making a difference and being a leader to those on your team. It took a reminder, but that's okay—the end result is the same. People are still bestowing the leader role upon you because of your actions.

Now be prepared, because there will come an amazing and completely unpublicized day when doing this becomes a part of who you are, and you'll no longer require external motivation. A moment where it's woven into the fabric of your being, now an inseparable part of your genetic makeup. The day this happens, you've reached leader criticality, and your life will never be the same.

*\*\**

Like every other leader, I can't pinpoint the day I went critical. I'm pretty certain it happened sometime in 2020, the year I took my first formal management position. But to be clear, I didn't go *leader critical* because I got a job with functional authority. In fact, in a toxic work environment produced by my boss, my job duties meant I was constantly having to protect those who reported to me. Not physically, but I needed to ensure they weren't getting passed over for promotions, screwed over in yearly assessments, or treated as disposable objects within our organization. Being in this setting flipped a switch in my brain.

Up to that point, I knew that teams were successful when people were successful. I knew that by helping everyone around me, we as a team would get better. And that in order for members of the team to reach their potential, they needed to first have their basic needs met. Yet, to be very candid, doing actions that facilitated this was not my default.

Of course, I wanted what was best for others, but up until 2020, I would still find myself having internal conversations—dilemmas—about who came first: Joe or the team. And it wasn't as though I had to decide whether to put my own personal survival needs on hold (I don't live in the Alaskan wilderness). It was things like, "Do I really have to help them with that? Can't they just figure it out?" or "Oh, that sounds messy, I think I'd rather keep to myself." Thoughts that don't make you a terrible person, just ones you have to fight through to become a leader. Those thoughts indicated I hadn't gone leader critical yet. That my default mode, my state of mind going into every encounter, wasn't that of a leader. And for the record, I don't expect you to be here yet. You're just starting out. In fact, there are countless leaders, maybe even ones that you look up to and respect, that have not gone critical yet.

Criticality is a big step, but reaching it doesn't mean you'll never make another mistake or do an action that isn't directly or indirectly helping you become a better leader. It's your state of mind. How you see and view the world. It's like shifting from a glass-half-empty to a glass-half-full kind of person. You can still drop or spill that glass, and in the process make quite a mess. But your entire outlook on the glass, the table, and the liquid inside is altered.

This is what I meant earlier when I said your entire life was about to change. Once you reach this point, when-ever that is and however it happens, you'll see the world differently. And it won't be until you stop, take a breath, and examine yourself as a leader that you'll realize it has occurred. There's no alert that goes off, and you don't get an email from the leader illuminati congratulating you on finally reaching this milestone. No, sadly, it is likely to hap-pen without you even realizing it. Others might recognize it in you, but internally, you'll feel the exact same. Except for one thing: helping others will now be your normal state. You might still have days where you're just not that into it—where you wake up and matters in your own life are tell-ing you to hit snooze five hundred more times—but once you get out of bed and into your day, *not* helping someone would actually require convincing in your brain. When this occurs, you've gone critical.

As you finish this book and progress in your leadership journey, here is one way to spot if it's happened: have a reg-ularly scheduled and extremely frank look at yourself. It's not fun, it may hurt a bit, but that's okay, as it will only make you a better leader. Being honest with yourself sucks. It's so much easier to just continue on in ignorant bliss. But if your goal is to be the best leader you can possibly be, these self-checks are a must.

Answer these honestly:

1.  Make a list of every person on a team you're a part of.
2.  When's the last time you went out of your way to help each person on that list?

Full stop.

Right now, in the middle of reading this list, pretend your phone buzzes, and it's someone from your team reaching out via text to let you know they're not doing well. What do you do?

Turn your phone over because this is "you time" and you're in the middle of something? Text back, but in thirty minutes after you've had a chance to accomplish some other house chores you wanted to get done today? Or pick up the phone and call the person to see how they're doing?

Leadership is rarely convenient. Being one can't be scheduled into a free one-hour block on your calendar. The scenarios that determine whether you're a great leader or just an average one will be thrown at you all day long. When it's not timely for you, when you haven't had a chance to prepare, and when you're least expecting it. How you respond in these moments determines whether you're a leader. Your outlook will let you know if you've gone critical.

# Chapter 25
## Checking In

Any moron can write a book. It's just words on pages. Writing one that's worth reading and will actually help you become a better leader—now there's a challenge.

Your goal is to become a leader, and mine is to help you accomplish that. Leaders have followers. It's a common and undisputed fact of leadership. Though, as I've already proven to you, it's more accurately stated this way: people follow leaders. Be someone others want to follow, someone they choose to follow, and boom—you're a leader.

But knowing all this information on leadership is one thing—applying it is another story.

# Chapter 26
## Balance

Despite my at times nerdy exterior, I have never once completed a Rubik's cube. Shocking, I know. I wish I could list it as an accomplishment, but sadly, I cannot. I've watched enough YouTube videos on the process to make me an expert, having seen them completed hundreds of times, yet for some reason I can't muster the expertise to do one myself. It's different when that six-sided plastic square is sitting in your meaty sausage fingers. That's the difference between theory and practice. How some ideas are great in theory, but in practice (their application out in the real world)—not so much. Less straightforward, less user-friendly, less *good*. Cooking is a lot like this as well. I can watch *Chopped* or the spiky bleached hair of Guy Fieri for hours, but the instant I throw an apron on, all bets are off. The exact opposite of what I want to happen here.

What I'm writing in this book actually works. It's worked for me, and I've seen it work for countless others. The biggest hurdle to overcome is recognizing that roles and functions are different. You're hired to functions, but you must earn roles. Functions are static, whereas roles can change, evolve, and disappear. Roles are what people consider you; functions are what is above your name in a conference call. As you go out and officially start your leadership journey, you are going to be handed a Rubik's cube leadership dilemma: How do I do both? How do I perform my functional duties and still act as a leader to others?

\*\*\*

There's an unexplainable moment of clarity right before an accident. Where carnage and solitude briefly intersect, silencing the clutter of life to illuminate what is otherwise invisible. It was during grad school that I experienced this phenomenon, a moment I will never forget. The tray was heavy (or maybe I'm just a wimp), and I was trying my best not to shake as I carefully traversed the minefield that was a packed restaurant. My large torso bent unnaturally to the right, my elbow and wrist dangerously close to dislocation. I don't remember exactly what caused the accident—an extended leg, a bump to the midsection, an uncontrollable sneeze—all I know is that in a split second, I was simultaneously yelling the F-word and launching overpriced entrées across the room.

An air raid of seafood pasta and abnormally large salads were sent hurling onto the floor in a slow-motion disaster worthy of a sitcom. A saucy explosion propelling noodles and leafy greens everywhere. And as the room fell instantly silent, with every eyeball laser-focused on me, I was given my moment of clarity: I should've taken that job at Target.

Looking back, I can't say I disagree with my former self. I was quite possibly one of the worst servers to ever wear a uniform. I didn't put the orders in to the kitchen correctly, I'd constantly forget drinks, and, for whatever reason, I could not seem to balance plates and glasses to save my soul. A normal human would expect that to be the easiest part of the job. Take the finished food from the kitchen and out to the hungry guests. A pretty straightforward task for someone with limbs. Yet this was the part of the job that gave me the most anxiety. I'm a decently athletic guy. I played sports growing up, and I'm still quasi-flexible and in seemingly decent shape for my age. And yet, for whatever reason, in those situations with the pressure on, I couldn't seem to find my balance. My trays were always shaking as they tilted dangerously from side to side. It's a miracle my tables ever had any food reach them at all. Life is all about balance, and I couldn't seem to find mine.

As a society, we're constantly stressing the importance of balance. We tell our children they need to be well-rounded individuals. School, sports, hobbies, music—a balance of breadth and mastery. As adults, it's the elusive work–life balance, trying to find the harmonious and impossibly small intersection where a successful career coexists with a perfect home life. Every day tipping the scales; every day a constant pursuit to bring them back into equilibrium. Our days are consumed by this quest to find balance—harmony—in every aspect of life.

It's the same reason our brains are drawn to complementary colors. Too much navy blue or bright orange on its own can be assaulting to the eyes, but when paired together from across the color wheel, we enjoy the combination. They balance each other out. That's why so many sports teams and businesses use this tactic for their logos. It's also the reason we find symmetry so appealing. We like symmetrical things and are constantly searching them out—faces, photographs, automobiles. The more balanced they are, the more enjoyable they are to look at. The importance of balance is engrained in us, which is why new leaders often mistakenly revert to this concept when they first start out. It's incorrectly thought that leadership is something to be balanced, and that there is a magical place—somewhere only the great leaders know about—where role and function balance each other perfectly.

This place does not exist.

# Chapter 27
## The Grand Canyon

My dad is an extremely intelligent and inquisitive person. He was a university tax and accounting professor, which should give you some insight into what our dinner conversations were like. "Joe, have you read the new tax code yet? It's about six hundred pages, but I think it's a pretty good read." Absolutely not, but I'm glad there are people out there who do find that sort of thing interesting (so the rest of us can continue on with literally anything else). Aside from his strange fascination with tax, he and my mom have always been incredibly supportive, which was exactly the case when I told them I was writing this book.

"Oh, that's great, Joey," my mom said, assuring me I'd be a bestseller before having ever written a word (classic mom). My parents both told me they were eager to read it once I was finished. They asked for an overview of my idea, which I gladly gave them, at which point my dad—who's always relating things to sports—posed a question that all new leaders need to hear. "So, what happens if you're the coach of a team, and two players want the same position, but only one of them can have it? How does your leadership theory handle that situation?"

The perfect question, and the type you will almost certainly be forced to navigate in the not-so-distant future. A relentless onslaught of difficult decisions that appear almost impossible to traverse while remaining a great leader. A point in the road where leadership and management (or whatever your functional duty is) appear to split apart and head in opposite directions, leaving a giant chasm in their wake. A moment where, unless you choose left or right, you will find yourself suspended in midair, doomed to free fall to the bottom.

***

As leaders, we serve two purposes on our team—our function (manager, director, engineer, coach, teacher, etc.) and our role (leader). And although they can seem worlds apart at times, it's crucial to recognize that we're actually both of these things, all the time. A leader and a coach—a leader and a teacher—a leader and an executive. Never *or*—always *and*. The trap new leaders fall into, and the same one I found myself stuck in when I first started, is to mistakenly think you must somehow divide your time between the two. That roles can't possibly be performed at the same time as functions, or vice versa. That there are moments when you shelve one for the other. "Dedicate four hours to management and then four hours to leadership." I can absolutely relate to this line of reasoning (and recognize why we default to it), but it's definitely wrong.

Treating the leader role like this will destine you to a lifetime of frustration, undue stress, and premature gray hairs. Not to mention that with this outlook, you'll continually let down your team, and I should know. I ran mine into the ground doing it this way and almost drove myself mad in the process. No matter how hard you may want to, you're not allowed to separate them. Doing so would mean there are times when you can put one ahead of the other, which isn't how it works.

There's only one real "rule" to keep in mind as I let you loose and out into the world after we finish here: you can never sacrifice one for the other, even when it's tempting to do so. And trust me, it's going to be.

***

There's a crispness in the air. Apple cider, baggy sweat-shirts, and pumpkin-spiced everything have officially kicked off the start of fall. Offspring are finally heading back to school, Halloween is on the horizon, and football season is once again upon us. And it's an especially exciting time for you and your family, since this is your first year as head coach of the Milliard University Mustangs.

All summer long, you've worked with your team—coaching, encouraging, and pushing them to their limits. Conditioning sessions at 6:00 a.m., strength training in the afternoons, and recently, a full two weeks of grueling practices—all in preparation for the first weekend in September, your first game. After a draining summer and a season that felt like it would never arrive, it's finally time to play against a real opponent. Which means setting a starting lineup—and ultimately, hurting some feelings in the process.

The rules of football state that only 11 players per team can be out on the field at a time. Meaning there are 22 starters (offense and defense), along with a handful of key backups to give them a rest, who will see considerable playing time during a game (let's put the total number at 30). However, most college teams consist of anywhere from 80 to 100 players (sometimes even more), meaning that, on average, only about 30 percent of the team will get to play during a game. Yes, there are some other ways to get guys on the field (punting, kicking, etc.), but most don't grow up wanting to play those positions. No, everybody wants to be a starter, and no position is more competitive than that of the quarterback (the one that throws the ball and gets all the glory).

Only one quarterback gets to play at a time, and they rarely ever sub themselves in and out for breaks like other positions do. Yet there are usually a handful of guys on the roster who all desperately want the job. Which is the exact predicament you find yourself in with your first game just one week away.

Cameron and Winston are two QBs on your team fighting for this coveted spot. Each has dedicated their entire summer to winning the position and made it very clear that being the starting quarterback is something they want. In a perfect world, both would get to play, and the Mustangs would win every game by fifty points. Unfortunately, that isn't reality. Most games are highly competitive, and you must put your best players on the field in hopes of edging out your opponent. Remember, the goal of any football team is winning games and ultimately, the championship. Success in this world is easily quantifiable and highly visible—how many wins did the team have? A winning record and your job is likely safe, while a losing one could put your function as head coach (and the paychecks that accompany it) in jeopardy.

Who you select to be your starting quarterback will have a direct impact on the outcome of your season. Both Cameron and Winston are exceptional athletes, and they bring unique attributes to the position. Ultimately though, you must make a decision on who will get to play. How you handle this situation will speak volumes about you as a coach, and as a leader.

*\*\*\**

Above all, the goal of a leader is their team's success. Good leaders recognize that in order for their team to be successful, the individual members of their team must therefore be successful. Facilitating this by helping them with their needs and wants, thereby making the team better—and in the process becoming someone they want to follow—is the heart of Leader Relativity. So, what happens when two people want the same thing?

Your goal is to support every member of your team. But in a resource-limited world (real life), you may be unable to facilitate this for everyone. This is where the interplay between functions and roles really comes to a head. The point in the road where new leaders look down and see nothing but a Grand Canyon–sized gap between being a leader and doing their job. An impasse where a decision must be made: Do I go left and continue as a leader, or right and fulfill my functional duties to the team? It's by far the most challenging moment for a new leader, and one that's rarely navigated correctly. Here are two of the most common responses to this ultimatum.

Hard-ass: The new leader takes a sharp right, putting their function ahead of being a leader and, in doing so, they revert to old, antiquated ideas about leadership. Many insecure first-time managers end up going this route. They think people won't listen to them or take them seriously unless they employ a "my way or the highway" approach. Difficult decisions are viewed as Band-Aids to be ripped off as quickly as possible to alleviate prolonged suffering. They mistakenly see kindness as weakness, and they are quick to insert themselves into situations that often don't require their input. They don't worry about how a message is communicated, only that it has the desired effect. In their function-focused heads, demeaning and empowering can accomplish the same thing.

It's a sad thing to see when a new leader goes this route, but believe it or not, becoming a hard-ass actually isn't the most common path people take when faced with the function–role fork in the road. More often than not, they head in the opposite direction, into the realm of people pleasing.

People Pleaser: The new leader goes left instead, thinking they must put aside their function on the team to ensure they don't hurt anyone's feelings. To them, the risk of ruffling feathers means jeopardizing the connection and relationship they've established with their team, so they back off from difficult decisions or challenging conversations. They end up fostering a "lead by committee" dynamic, where they (as the person with functional authority) get run over—eventually losing control of the entire team they've been entrusted with. New leaders that end up on this path often have high levels of empathy. It's hard for them to make someone uncomfortable, so they'd rather sacrifice something else (potentially the team's success) to ensure they don't hurt anyone's feelings. But leaders are not people pleasers, and this type of behavior doesn't do anyone any good—especially those who follow them.

For as simple as I've tried to make leadership in this book, the act of being a leader out in the real world, in coordination with your function, requires a great deal of nuance. And believe it or not, it's possible for people to find you unlikable in the moment but still consider you a leader worth following.

*\*\**

The goal of this book is to demystify leadership. To prove that becoming a leader is something anyone on earth, no matter how much power or status they have, can achieve. It's a pretty straightforward concept ($\blacksquare \rightarrow \odot$), but I don't want to give the illusion that leadership is shallow or in any way basic—a simple list of tasks to check off, which will in turn make you someone people want to follow. It's a lot more than that. There's subtlety involved. Yes, you are helping others with their needs and wants, but there are many different paths you can take to accomplish this.

At times, it's a straight line: "I need something"—fulfill need; "I want something"—fulfill want. An analogous situation I encounter as a manager that follows this line of reasoning is "I want a promotion"—I agree that you're doing amazing work and should be compensated accordingly—I submit paperwork for the promotion. As straightforward as it gets. Someone wants something, and I'm able to facilitate it. They've shown they are great at their job and deserving of a promotion. Piece of cake, and my heart rate doesn't exceed seventy beats per minute. As a manager and a leader, I love when this happens—a direct route to helping a follower. It aligns with our team's success, and it is something I'm able to accommodate. But as much as I enjoy it when this happens, these situations are akin to winning a scratch-off ticket. Not impossible, but certainly rarer than you'd like.

You will find that a much more involved and winding path must usually be taken to help someone with their L1 and L2. That's because we always have our functional duties that we must perform at the same time. Unfortunately, as a manager, I simply can't give a promotion to every member of my team every day; that would be unrealistic for a host of reasons. Often, it's because that person hasn't proven to me that they're ready to take the next step in their career and assume more responsibilities on the team. It's right here that many new leaders assume there are only two choices available: hurt the person's feelings and shut down their hopes of advancement, or give in to their request so they will continue to like you and therefore follow you. Two paths, light-years apart from one another, constructed by our brains when we don't understand the nuances of the leader role.

The shortest distance between two objects is a straight line. Not only does it get us to our destination the fastest, but it's by far the easiest route to picture in our heads. And when this path is blocked or unavailable to us, we momentarily short-circuit and jump to this incorrect conclusion: A follower wants something—for whatever reason, I'm unable to fulfill it—they'll no longer consider me someone they want to follow—leadership fail. But this actually isn't what happens.

Remember, people follow you because it's in their best interest, not because they like you. Sure, that's a nice thing to have—and being kind, empathetic, and respectful will often make you someone they genuinely enjoy being around—but ultimately, that isn't what they're after as a follower. They want their human needs and wants satisfied, and they're choosing to follow you because you actually care about them as a person and are willing to actively help in that pursuit. The key word there being *help*. You're supporting them on their way, not doing it for them.

If someone wants a promotion and they're not ready, I'll often start the conversation by discussing what an advancement in their role would look like: expertise, skill sets, and responsibilities that are required from that function. Then I mention that before I can place someone into this position, I need previous examples proving they're capable of taking it on. At which point I might say, "I know this is something you really want and are passionate about, and although I don't think you're ready to take that step today, it doesn't mean we can't make it a goal of ours to work toward. Let's you and I talk through a plan for how we can get you there." Then we sit down and identify areas where they need improvement and avenues for addressing those skill sets. The result of that conversation (which will always make me sweat no matter how often I have them) is me telling them they aren't ready, but how I go about delivering that message is what allows me to remain both a manager and a leader at the same time, and avoid tumbling into the Grand Canyon.

Deep down, I want them to succeed, so I am always coming up with new ways for that to happen. And sure, they may not agree with my assessment, but after that conversation, there's no denying that I actually want to support them in their pursuit. The road to becoming a great leader is riddled with difficult decisions and uncomfortable discussions, but it's just as much how you go about doing something as it is what you're actually doing. Condescending and motivating can each get someone to perform better; one makes you an ass, while the other makes you a leader.

＊＊＊

I'm making an omelet and I need to break a few eggs. Luckily for me, I've got options. I can tap the egg against the side of a bowl and carefully separate it from the shell, or take out a sledgehammer and blow it to smithereens. Either way, I've cracked the egg, but with two very different methods.

Navigating difficult situations (and the conversations that accompany them) is part of leadership. A lack of confidence, along with unrefined communication skills, create the function-role ultimatum in the heads of so many at the first sign of turbulence. The "easy routes" are clearly paved and readily discernible, which can fool anyone into thinking they're the only options available. In reality, there are millions of paths at any given moment that allow you to be both a leader and a manager—a leader and a coach—a leader and a *(blank)*—at the same time. Luckily, most of us are already versed in how to do this; we just don't recognize it.

If you've ever had to employ "tough love" with a friend or family member, then you're already a professional in how to navigate these types of situations. Tough love is what happens when you truly care about someone but disagree with them on an important subject—usually around their actions or behaviors. A friend in a toxic relationship or a loved one with self-destructive behaviors are two instances where tough love is commonly employed. But what makes a conversation *tough love* isn't just the result of the interaction, but rather the messaging used.

Because you care about the person, you bring up your concerns delicately and with significant thought and consideration beforehand. You don't storm into the room and say, "Hey listen up, moron, here are all the reasons you're wrong. Sit tight, it's a long list." Of course not. You take a less direct route while still getting to the same destination. "Kim, I know you've been going through some things lately, but I'd like to discuss some of your recent behaviors. I don't think you mean to, but you're hurting those around you. We know this is a sensitive subject, so please recognize we are only saying something because we really care about you." A delicate dance of empathy, respect, and concern. And the skills used to have a tough love conversation are the exact same ones we leverage when the leader–manager chasm starts rearing its ugly head.

Remember, there's always an option C, an option D, an option E, that will allow you to remain both a manager and a leader. You just need the vision to find it and the confidence to take it. And let's get one thing clear—you're going to screw this up in the beginning—and that's okay. These situations require practice to get good at. In fact, I still mess them up and I'm writing the book on it. Nobody is perfect, but it's okay—because people understand you're human and that you'll make mistakes. The most important thing is that you understand this too and don't beat yourself up over it. Nobody has a magic playbook that tells them exactly what to say in every scenario. That would be awesome and would alleviate a lot of the stress, but it doesn't exist. The more you do this, the easier finding alternate paths will be for you, and you'll be better suited to have those conversations.

\*\*\*

Another common scenario emerging leaders find themselves in as they gain positions of functional authority is when someone on the team is underachieving. It's a classic lose–lose scenario on the surface, and one that is sure to cause stress and anxiety when you first come across it (whether you're managing a team of engineers, or coaching a football team and having to select a quarterback).

\*\*\*

Your team, the Milliard Mustangs, is seven days away from its first game, and the time has come to finalize who will be your starting quarterback. Both Cameron and Winston are good students with positive attitudes and exceptional work ethics. They're good teammates and have spent the entire off-season in preparation to become the starting quarterback. However, on the field, Cameron is simply a better player than Winston.

He has a stronger arm, he's a more accurate passer, and his decision-making skills always put the offense in a better position to move the ball down the field. It's clear to everyone that Cameron is physically and mentally a better football player, which is why you know you will select him as your starter. Therefore, you must also break the news to Winston that he will begin the season as the backup.

You tell Winston to stop by your office before he heads home after practice, and as you do, your palms are already starting to sweat. You're about to embark on a part of the job no coach enjoys, though one that must be done. But you recognize that you can still be a leader in difficult times.

"Hey Winston, please have a seat. I know playing quarterback at Milliard has been a goal of yours for a while. And we all recognize the amount of time you've put in this off-season to improving your skills and becoming a better ballplayer. However, at this time, I think Cameron gives us the best opportunity to be successful as a team and to run our offense, so I've chosen him to be our starting quarterback. Now, that's not to say you aren't still a valuable part of this team, or that there won't still come a day where we rely on you to win games—it just means right now we'll have you on the bench instead of on the field. I know being our quarterback is something you're passionate about, and I think it's a goal you can still accomplish during your time here. There are some areas of your game that need a bit more work, but with enough practice, I know you can take your game to the next level . . ."

The conversation continues with you highlighting areas for improvement and then giving Winston a chance to comment on the situation. Although disappointed in the result, Winston leaves the meeting optimistic—as opposed to dejected—because it was made clear that he is a valued and respected member of the team.

Now, had you gone into that conversation and simply said, "Sorry Winston, you're just not that good and we're going to bench you. You'll need to get a lot better before this is even a topic worth bringing up again. See you at practice," that would've crushed him and certainly given him the impression that you really don't give a sh*t about him or his career. But you didn't do that. As a leader, you ultimately want every member of your team to succeed, because that's how the team succeeds.

Thankfully for the Mustang players and staff, you recognize that you're always a leader and a coach, to everyone on your team, all the time. So, the first time you find yourself staring straight down into the leader–function void, I want you to jump. Close your eyes, bend your knees, and do what feels like the impossible. You may scrape your knee and stumble over your words from time to time, but I promise you, there is solid ground there.

# Chapter 28
## Under Pressure

Every day I get a little older. Aching joints, a little less on top, and random hairs poking out from new places constantly—aging is one of life's great mysteries. Which undiscovered body part will hurt tomorrow? How many times will I complain that kids these days just don't get it? The classic signs of early onset "old-man-ism" are already starting to show. And the older I get, the more I've come to appreciate old boring sayings that I used to shrug off. Mainly because as I age, I realize how many of them are true (which is probably why they became sayings in the first place). One that's caught my attention lately is that "pressure breaks pipes, but also makes diamonds."

When my wife and I first moved into our house, the water pressure was through the roof. Our shower could've power washed the skin off my scalp, it was so high—which was great for household chores but terrible for our water lines. The home inspector told us we needed to decrease it or else it may cause a leak in the future. We have since lowered it to a normal level, and I'm happy to say I still have all my skin, but it's not just the physical piping that feels the stresses of pressure. The fluids in them undergo changes as well: flow rate, viscosity, and even the temperature of a liquid are altered when pressurized. For example, the boiling point of water at sea level (1 atm of pressure) is 212°F; however, inside a pipe with a pressure of 200 atm, the boiling point increases to 328°F. Pressure can cook a pot roast in thirty-five minutes, and over billions of years, it can turn carbon molecules into diamonds. Pressure changes things, and people are no exception.

Being a leader is pretty straightforward when things are going well—when there's no turmoil on the team and work deliverables are being met. It's a completely different story when that isn't the case. The philosopher and former heavyweight boxer Mike Tyson once famously said, "Everyone has a plan until they're punched in the face." Well, in our case, the saying would be "Everyone can be uplifting and empowering when things are going good." The true test for any leader is how they handle adversity.

Understaffed, behind schedule, and resource-limited. These are the telltale signs that things aren't going well, and they're usually the moments when the pressures of our functional duties (work) start weighing on us. How we respond, and how we continue to treat others on our team, speak volumes about the type of leader we are. The bad ones succumb to it. They use it to justify being crappy to those around them because they're simply under too much pressure to give people the time and decency they deserve—which is absolute BS. Please don't let this happen to you.

Stress is no excuse to put being a leader on pause, to stop supporting and serving those around you. Remember, people can only succeed and make your team better when their needs are being met. If you put their L1 on hold (which includes emotional and mental well-being), then their ability to contribute to the team is put on hold as well. Your stress will actually increase as a result of this behavior, because the members of your team will become less productive. In other words, be a sh*t-head to people, and you get what you deserve—more stress.

And I think it's fair to say that most new leaders don't do this maliciously. However, in their pursuit of making the team better and increasing the productivity of its members, they become demeaning because of the stress instead of what they're really after: elevating and empowering. They become sharp, short, and cold in their interactions as their body initiates survival mode to cope with the stress.

And I'm well aware of how tempting it is to get like this with coworkers as your own stress builds. Everyone feels the urge—it's human nature. We unconsciously shut down all auxiliary efforts and focus solely on ourselves. It's a form of fight or flight, and when we do this, we inevitably become impatient with and detached from those around us. All leaders feel this at some point, but the good ones don't let it overtake them. They're able to effectively handle the stress and still be a leader to their team. One strategy I've found that works for me is to label the feeling when I start noticing it in myself. Having enough self-awareness to recognize the pressure means I can take action to prevent it from negatively influencing my actions (causing me to become a jerk).

Sometimes I tell myself, "Buck up Joey, your team needs you. It's not their fault you feel like a skyscraper is sitting on your chest. They deserve better." So I force a smile and continue with my day. Sometimes I'll even go out of my way to consciously act like the "regular" version of myself. The cheery, inquisitive, and often silly form of Joe that they are used to. It's not at all how I'm feeling in the moment, but I know that doing so can get me through a rough patch of the day and ensure nobody thinks that what I'm feeling is directed at them—which is an unintended consequence of getting into a stress-induced rut.

And other times—to be quite candid—when I'm having an extremely rough day (which we all have from time to time), I'll just cancel a meeting with someone. If I know that I'm in such a rotten headspace that no matter how hard I try, I won't be able to fake it (and I'd possibly risk being a terrible leader to that person), I reschedule the interaction to later in the day, or tomorrow. It doesn't make me weak or any less of a leader; it just makes me human. Now, putting off every meeting clearly isn't the answer, but we all know ourselves, and if you're not okay to chat, then you're not okay to chat—and that's fine. Recognizing it's happening is half the battle. If you don't know something is off, you'll continue with business as usual and likely revert to old habits. Great leaders make an effort to course correct, or cool off, before holding their followers accountable for the stresses of their own life. It's true that pressure breaks pipes, along with inexperienced leaders.

\*\*\*

Leadership isn't about you. It's a bit harsh when phrased like that, but it's true. People follow other people because they choose to, because they want help in getting their own needs and wants met. I'm not saying you can't be human and express emotion, but rather that you need to remember that what you're feeling isn't their fault, so don't treat them like it is. Being a leader is tough. The examples I just gave are realistic; sometimes performing your functional duties kind of sucks—it happens. But you're still a leader to your team that day whether you feel up to it or not, whether things are going good, bad, or in between.

As you progress in your career, you'll find your own groove and come up with your own methods for handling these situations. You'll have a backlog of experience to refer to on how to effectively cope with stress. You'll know how your body and mind react in these moments, and you'll eventually find them easier to navigate as you grow both in your function and as a leader—simultaneously. Which is why, no matter how you slice it, I think being a frontline manager with other people reporting to you is one of the most difficult jobs out there.

\*\*\*

Last month, someone asked what my favorite part of my job was. It took me all of three milliseconds to respond back with "Seeing other people become leaders." And it's absolutely true; there's nothing better than helping someone find their leadership wings and then releasing them into the wild to be a life-changing leader for countless others. It's why I wrote this book and why I try to mentor as many people as I possibly can.

Recently, I've been coaching a young woman at work (we'll call her Tab) who has expressed interest in becoming a leader. Tab has the potential to one day be a great leader and manager. Cares about others, driven, detail-oriented with a team-first mentality—she's well on her way. As often as possible, I try to delegate managerial duties to Tab so she can get a taste of what the day-to-day of a manager looks like. I also constantly sprinkle in advice and walk her through how I go about leading the team, not just managing it—and putting her in positions to do the same. She's done an amazing job since joining the team, but it wasn't until a recent career discussion that Tab perfectly, and unknowingly, summed up the disconnect that new leaders are feeling.

"You know, Joe, I'm certain I want to one day become a manager, but I'm not sure if I want to be a *people manager* or a *program manager*." My jaw hit the floor. With that one brief and perfect sentence, I felt instantly vindicated for writing this book, but the words also sent shivers down my spine. Tab confirmed that this is the message we're putting into the heads of prospective leaders—that you either lead people or manage programs—not both. And I know exactly where this is coming from.

It's no secret that being both a manager and a leader is difficult. It's so tough, in fact, that companies have invented a job specifically to combat the issue. Instead of trying to coach aspiring leaders through the process, they've instead taken the easy route and created a position that has all the functional duties of a manager but aims to alleviate the leadership aspect of it: the program manager.

It's a position of functional authority, and one that has all the responsibilities of a manager, yet nobody reports to them. They have nobody on their "desktop." Nobody has them as a "reports to manager." When viewed on an org chart, they appear as a little floaty head with nobody under them. This is intentional, and it revolves around the misconceived idea companies have that leadership and a management are to somehow be balanced during the day, unable to coexist with one another. A sentiment which we now know to be false.

The issue stems from one thing—results—which, really, is money. The companies we work for have a bottom line that must be reached for them to stay afloat and thereby keep us employed. Generate revenue and pay employees—that is corporations in a nutshell. And they all have managers. They're the ones on the front lines ensuring deadlines are being met and programs are running smoothly, while constantly connecting the dots between the executives and the workforce (those actually doing the work). Managers are where the rubber meets the road. They handle staffing plans, assign resources, and perform a host of other functional duties that ensure their teams are staying productive. Which is why so many organizations have fallen prey to thinking that being a leader is bogging down their managers, so why not just remove it from their job description entirely by not having them "own" anyone?

Well, for starters, the idea that managers own people is horribly off base. It gives the illusion that you can treat the people who report to you as objects. Things to be used and leveraged instead of living, breathing people. Anytime I hear another manager or executive at work use the word "own" when it comes to employees, I immediately think to myself, "Well, there's someone that doesn't get it." I own a car. I also own my own home. Neither of those objects follow me around or look to me for guidance or inspiration during the day. I could treat my car like crap and leave ten fish tacos in the back seat for a week, completely neglecting it, and it will still be my car when I return. Disgusting? Yes. But the next time I get in and fire it up, it will be like nothing ever happened (minus the smell).

The people who choose to follow us don't owe you and me anything. A car is supposed to start when you put in the key. And if I sell my car, it will work the exact same when the next person goes to drive it. That's the hallmark of an automobile, or anything else you may own, yet it has nothing in common with leadership. To own an employee is an antiquated idea, and one that eventually leads to the down-fall of any organization. When executives try to shield their managers from the growing pains associated with per-forming functional duties in parallel with leadership, their companies crumble from the bottom up.

I finished my conversation with Tab by telling her that being a great leader can at times be difficult. You have to perform your functional duties as a manager and at the same time continue to be a leader to those on your team. I told her it's so difficult that our company has tried to alle-viate the leadership aspect completely and just focus on delivering results. Here's hoping she decides to take on the challenge of being both.

# Chapter 29
## There Is No Mold

Two pirates, Davy and Dewey, meet in a local bar. Dewey has a patch over one eye, a hook for a hand, and a wooden peg leg. "Avast ye, matey," exclaims Davy as they sit down. "What happened to ya?"

Dewey says, "Me pirate ship was attacked, and a lucky shot lopped off me leg. So now I got me a wooden peg."

"And your hand?" asks Davy.

"When me ship sank, a shark bit it clean off. So now I got me a hook for a hand."

"Okay, that makes sense, but what's with the eye patch?"

"I was mindin' me own business standin' on the dock, when the biggest seagull I ever saw flies overhead and poops right in me eye."

"But ya don't go blind from seagull poop," Davy says, confused.

"True," says Dewey. "But it was me first day with the hook."

The man who told a joke much like this one wasn't sitting around with friends playing poker, or on a beach sipping a margarita. Rather, picture yourself in a hot telegraph room at 2:00 a.m. anxiously awaiting updates from the battlefield, the tension so thick you could cut with a knife. And believe it or not, this dad-joke cracking speaker would also go on to deliver one of the most momentous decrees in the last two hundred years, the Emancipation Proclamation, as well as give one of the most moving speeches ever recited—the Gettysburg Address. Abraham Lincoln, one of America's greatest presidents and adored leaders, never wavered from his personality as a humorist and a storyteller.

Even in moments of extreme tension, old Abe always had his wits about him and used his sense of humor to diffuse situations—putting others, and himself, at ease. This joke is the exact type of humor Abe leveraged on a daily basis and in moments you wouldn't expect. (Of course, this a modern example since the jokes from 1860 haven't aged well.) Certainly not the type of story you'd expect to hear from a president alive during a civil war and now permanently enshrined on Mount Rushmore. Picturing someone more stoic and less jovial? I'm telling you, there is no mold for being a leader. Anyone on earth can do it.

Whatever your personality is right now, in this exact moment, will be just fine for leading others. In fact, it's perfect. There are zero requirements on demeanor, speaking styles, or any of the other personal character qualities we so often (and incorrectly) associate with being a leader. There's a terribly outdated saying that "There's more than one way to skin a cat." We are animal lovers here, so all cats, dogs, and other exotic pets (the type that are red flags on first dates) are safe here. But the saying is fitting; there is more than one way to be a leader. Billions, in fact.

What I've described in this book is all you have to do to become a leader. And nowhere did I state exactly how you should go about doing those things. That's the beauty of it. It's open to interpretation how you implement them. I often hear *Anyone can be a leader*. Well, if that's true, then any personality should be able to do it. Now clearly, being a narcissistic jerk won't cut it, but if that's someone's natural demeanor, they won't be able to support the people on their team—thereby disqualifying them from ever earning the leader role. As long as you aren't *that*, you can absolutely become a leader, exactly as you are today.

*\*\*

What do Natalie Portman, Albert Einstein, Lady Gaga, Sonia Sotomayor, and Tom Hanks all have in common? They're experts in their craft who have publicly acknowledged their impostor syndrome. That ugly sensation that puts our nerves on edge and tells us we're not worthy of our accomplishments or status. "One day someone will find out that I'm a fraud, that I don't actually know what I'm doing." If you ever find yourself feeling this way on your leadership journey, just remember that it's totally normal (if Tom and Gaga feel it, it must be). But ask yourself, *Am I nervous because of my function, or my role on the team as a leader?* The answer might help put you at ease.

When I took my first job in management, I had no idea what I was doing. And I can't stress that enough: absolutely zero intuition. My impostor syndrome score was through the roof for that entire first year.

"Joe, can you make us a staffing plan?"—I doubt it.

"Joe, do you have those earned value metrics ready for review?"—I think so?

"Joe, when do you think you'll have the subcontract with our supplier definitized?"—honestly, maybe never.

None of it felt natural to me because I had never done it before. But when I look back on that first year, everything that made me doubt myself had to do with my functional duties on the team. Responsibilities of mine that I wasn't an expert in. A fake-it-till-you-make-it mentality with countless Google searches and YouTube tutorials. My daily interactions with the team were the only place I ever felt comfortable, which I now understand was me fulfilling my role as a leader. "You need help with something? Easy, I can do that."

Should you ever find yourself feeling like an impostor, just ask yourself what it is about your current situation that you are finding the most difficult to justify. I'll bet the leader aspect isn't the culprit. And if by some chance it is, just remember, literally anyone on earth can be a leader. "But Joe, I'm not special. I can't be an amazing leader." I agree with you—you're not special. And you don't have to be. Upright and human—that's all it takes. Meet that "requirement" and you're set. Nothing special required.

# Chapter 30
## We're People Too

Every time I do it, it feels wrong. In fact, I'm cringing now just thinking about it. It's probably best described as downright disgusting, and anyone that likes it is certifiably deranged. And yet, you almost can't escape it. Spend enough time in the kitchen, and unless you're not a meat eater, you are eventually going to prepare a dish that calls for chicken—and in the process go skin to skin with that cold, slippery, slimy raw meat. One of the most unnatural and least enjoyable feelings in the world. Nothing else we touch can mimic this horrific texture. It's wet, it's squishy, it's miles away from being a spicy sandwich at this point. Uncooked chicken just isn't right.

It rivals one of my other least favorite things on earth—stepping out of the shower having forgotten my towel. Is there anything more unnatural than prancing around the house sopping wet? And even though monkeys creep me out, here is perhaps one of the most appropriate GIFs of all time:

Thankfully, these situations don't arise often, which is good news because of how unnatural they make us feel. They go against what our minds conceive as normal. These are just two examples, but there are countless others we encounter that our brains may identify as not quite right: vegan cheese, dessert before dinner, and hairless cats. These examples are the best way to describe how I answer this repeatedly posed question, and one that's usually on everyone's mind at this point: "So what happens if you have a bad manager, someone that's not a good leader?" It's a circumstance often referred to as *leading up*, and it is one of the most unnatural things a person can do on their team.

There's an unwritten assumption we all have: that those in positions of functional authority are going to be good leaders. We now recognize this isn't the case, since functions and roles are separate, but most of us just expect that our boss will be versed in leadership. It's the default outlook at any job. And yet, as we can all attest, this is absolutely not guaranteed to be the case. Bad leaders seem to always be around the corner, and they come in two flavors: indifferent and assholes. It's important to recognize which one you've got before deciphering how to take action.

***

My first boss after college (we'll call him Matt) was not a good leader, but he wasn't a jerk. For whatever reason, he just did not care. Apathetic toward other humans and making small talk when required, but completely uninterested in the details of other people's lives. He'd ask how you were, but you could see he was eager for you to finish talking so he could move the conversation on to work topics. Matt was the most common type of poor leader—indifferent. Not degrading, demeaning, or worthy of reporting to HR, just someone in a position of power that has zero interest in the human aspect of leadership (the only aspect). Nice enough folks, but in their minds, leadership has to do with one thing—productivity. Period.

They view leadership and their functional duty on the team as synonymous, and never come to the realization that the teams they oversee are full of individuals. There are a host of reasons this can happen (their own experiences, how they were taught, being uncomfortable having $L_1$ and $L_2$ conversations), but the end result is always the same—you find yourself with a poor leader.

Normally, as leaders, our interactions with the team are follower focused. Leadership isn't about us, so this makes sense; it's their lives, their needs, and their wants. So when you have an indifferent boss (and since you yourself are a good leader), your conversations with them will start to skew. As leading up starts to occur, you'll notice a seismic shift in your interactions with folks like Matt.

They'll resemble the exchanges you have with other members of your team, except now it's with someone who has more authority than you do. You start asking how they're doing (and caring about the answer). You inquire about their real life and see if there are places you can support them, even asking them career progression questions (normally an unusual conversation for an employee to have with their boss). Once this happens on a consistent basis, and you feel like you are more invested in their life than they are in yours, you are more often than not leading up—and thereby plunging your hands into a big bowl of raw chicken.

In the process of leading up, you'll start to gain influence with your boss. They may come to you for opinions on matters you would otherwise not expect them to. This is a classic sign that they now see you as a leader (whether they recognize it's happening or not). Even though becoming a leader doesn't make someone a genius, our teammates (and our boss is a member of the team) are constantly searching for support with their $L_1$ and $L_2$, and your boss is no different. If you seem like someone that can help, they will keep coming back to you for your input because doing so is advantageous for them as a human.

Leader Relativity governs every leadership dynamic ($\blacksquare \rightarrow \odot$) on the planet, and it doesn't care if $\odot$ is a manager with twenty years of experience or an employee early in their career. But it also doesn't restrict who ■ is either. Bosses and employees often establish and maintain ■ → ☉, and there's no requirement on who's who in this relationship. Behave in a way that makes others want to follow you, and you're a leader. Do that with your boss, and you're officially leading up.

*\*\*\**

Horseflies are hands down the worst creatures on this planet. Sure, we may dislike snakes, alligators, and spiders, but those are well-established feuds dating back thousands of years. I consider myself a spider assassin, and they know that if we cross paths, it's all-out war. But horseflies are different. We don't think about them, so for the most part, they're completely off our radar. That is, until we find ourselves peacefully enjoying the outdoors, completely minding our own business, when we are abruptly made aware of their existence through an excruciating bite. How can you not hate this insect? Their existence makes me mad and sad at the same time, and that is why I compare asshole leaders to them.

There's a senior manager at my work that is the epitome of a horsefly manager. A straight up, no-questions-about-it, call-it-like-you-see-it ass. We'll call them Taylor, and Taylor is the worst. They've had three ethics investigations conducted on them, and the attrition rate from their team must be hovering around 50 percent.

People despise working for them, and having spent time on a team with Taylor myself, I can concur—the stories are true. And should you find yourself with a Taylor of your own—a manipulative slimeball—it's important that you remember: as leaders, we're people too.

There's no rule that dictates *Thou shall attempt to lead up thy boss no matter the circumstance.* If you report to someone like Taylor, my advice is very simple—leave.

As a leader, there's no "code" you must uphold when in a horsefly situation. Yes, you want what's best for your terrible boss, but you're a person too. You won't find the "Be a perfect leader" spiel in here telling you how important it is to lead toxic people. Yes, there will be times when you have to lead those you dislike or disagree with, but that's different from what we're talking about here. If your Levels 1 and 2 are not being met (and reporting to a Taylor would do that), then you have to do what's best for you.

Sometimes I hear from people I consider to be good leaders who are stuck in situations like this, and I always tell them the same thing—it's okay to be human. When a horsefly descends upon your picnic, leaving really is the only option. Sure, you could sit there and get repeatedly bitten ten thousand times—but why would you do that? There are plenty of other places to have an amazing lunch.

# Chapter 31
## Leaving the Nest

"What just happened? We're done already? I can't believe it, that was so simple and painless."

I know.

Just like that, you're now ready to go out and become an extraordinary leader. There's clearly a lot we didn't cover, but that's okay because I gave you exactly what you need to become a leader—no more and no less. Sure, we could spend a hundred more pages on the nuance and psychology of why this works, with more drawn-out examples, but you don't need it. You (and I) have better things to do—like actually going out and leading our teams.

At this point, as I push you out of the nest and into the real world, you have a special power that not many possess: you actually know what leadership is. But with great power comes great responsibility. So I'm going to challenge you today—spread this idea of leadership (maybe even the book itself) to someone that's new to leadership and secretly guarding their own tiny leadership flame. Because the takeaway from this book needs to be shared: regardless of a person's age, job title, years of experience, or the amount of power they may have—anyone can become a leader once they know what it means to truly follow someone else.

So, as you go out and grow into the amazing leader you were meant to be, always remember: people will walk through fire to follow you if they know you truly care about them. That's what leadership is. And that's who your team needs you to be.

# Q&A

**I want to get into a leadership position at work. What's the best way to go about doing that?**

Remember, there are no "leadership positions" on any team. You can't apply to be a leader; that is a role that anyone with any functional duty is able to earn. But if you're interested in a career in management, I would suggest first and foremost letting your boss know and asking them about the path they took. Then go find other managers, coaches, etc. and ask how they did it. From there, you can assess your current position and how best to acquire the function you'd like. But no matter what your job title is or where you are in your organization, you can be an outstanding leader at this moment—that's the beauty of Leader Relativity.

**I work remotely, with most of my interactions happening over email, phone, and video conferencing. Can I still be a leader?**

Absolutely. In fact, I work on a hybrid team right now, with a good portion of my interactions happening over the internet or phone. The biggest hurdle I've found is that when working remotely, you no longer have the one-off conversations at the coffee maker to ask how someone is doing or pick their brain about life in general. You now must dedicate time and make a conscious effort to pick up the phone (or stay late on a Zoom call) to have those L1 and L2 types of interactions. It is absolutely possible to build a connection and help someone with their needs and wants when working remotely; it just takes a more concerted effort to find the time.

**What do you recommend as the next book to read after *Leader Relativity*?**

The three books I have been recommending for years to new leaders are *Dare to Lead* by Brené Brown, *Leaders Eat Last* by Simon Sinek, and *Extreme Ownership* by Jacko Willink. And even if you've read one of these before, I would bet if you reread them now, they would take on a different meaning.

**Who's your favorite leader of all time?**

If you couldn't tell, I'm partial to Abraham Lincoln. Reading about Abe's jovial and silly personality really opened my eyes to the fact that anyone can be a great leader and that there isn't a one-size-fits-all mold we have to adhere to. Also, Lincoln was a master at being a leader and a president (his functional duty on the United States team), never sacrificing one for the other. The book *Team of Rivals* by Doris Kearns Goodwin is a beautifully written biography on Lincoln, and it provides a master class on how to lead people you don't get along with.

**I'm midway through my career. Is it too late for me to become a leader?**

It's never too late! Anyone can become a great leader at any moment, and there certainly isn't an age or experience requirement (on either end of the spectrum). I think what most people get hung up on is, "Well, for better or worse, this is who I am now." If you haven't been acting like a leader for the first ten years of your career, that's okay. Start your next ten today with a different mindset. I'm always shocked (and saddened) when people tell me they wish they could change and be something different from what they are currently. It might feel weird at first if this isn't the norm for you, but just go with it. I promise you it will work.

**In your opinion, what's the hardest part about being a leader?**

Doing both your function and the leader role at the same time. The Grand Canyon dilemma is very real, and I still feel it almost daily.

**Is this really all it takes to be a leader? No formal training or degree required?**

None. Zero. Just however long it takes to read this book and learn the absolute basics. Training is great for functional duties but is absolutely not required for being a leader. You don't need a certificate or piece of paper to support other human beings and have them consider you a leader and someone worth following.

**How can I promote this style of leadership where I work?**

Be this type of leader, set an example for others, and teach it every chance you get. I can't stress enough how important it is that we, as leaders, grow other leaders. I didn't dedicate a section to it (as you are just starting out), but when you get more comfortable as a leader, I would encourage you to mentor other emerging leaders and share this mentality with them. It's the only way we all end up with better leaders in the future, and who doesn't want that?

**How do you manage and lead people that are your friends?**

> Very carefully. We are always both our function and our role, but it's especially difficult to do this when the members of your team are already your friends. Many new to leadership will default to putting their managerial duties on hold (turning a blind eye, putting off tough conversations, etc.) because they don't want to hurt someone's feelings and jeopardize that friendship. If done correctly and with great care, you can actually grow an even stronger relationship, but it isn't easy. You have to make it blatantly obvious that you care about them so that whatever actions are required as a part of your function (especially the difficult ones) aren't seen as personal.

**What's your favorite leadership quote?**

> "You manage things; you lead people."
> —Rear Admiral Grace Murray Hopper.

# Extras

I purposely wrote *Leader Relativity* to be read like a conversation. I don't like different sized text and random bold sayings because they're annoying and distracting—but here is a collection of things I wanted to add that either didn't quite have a home, or that I wanted to reiterate one last time.

- Most of us have no idea what we're doing. Treating people right is a great default and will get you 95 percent of the way to being a great leader.
- Reading this book makes you no more of a leader than a hermit without the internet. Leadership is not a passive activity; you actually have to go out and earn the leader role from everyone around you—all the time. Knowing what to do is one thing—actually doing it is another.
- The higher up you go in an organization, the harder it seems to lead—which results from not understanding how indirect actions work. Here's a test: if you can't name your company's CEO (or picture what they look like), then they are doing a poor job of leading your team, and they likely don't realize how to leverage indirect actions.

- As leaders, we're not trying to change people, but simply to support them. We accept our team members as they are, but we want them to be the best versions of themselves.

- It's absolutely possible to lead people you don't like personally or those you fundamentally disagree with on certain topics. As long as respect is maintained, there is no reason you can't lead someone vastly different from yourself.

- I've heard it said that "Confidence is the most important quality in a leader." No, it's not. Extreme self-doubt doesn't do you any favors, but an average amount of confidence will do you just fine.

- I almost compared leadership to gravity at one point—since when a great leader on your team walks in the room, you can feel it—but that isn't correct. Planets don't get to choose which celestial bodies they orbit—gravity just sort of sucks them in, and there they stay. What actually happens when a great leader walks in the room is that they have accrued so much influence and respect (which is noticeable to other members of the team) that they appear to have "gravity." In reality, this is a leadership reputation they have built that now precedes them when they walk into a room.

- Leadership has nothing to do with a person's inherent traits. Nobody is born a leader.

- Being vulnerable makes you relatable, which is a major reason why executives have such a hard time connecting with the people that work for them. If people can't relate to you, your life, your background, or your current circumstances, it will be incredibly hard to connect with them.

- Establishing a safe environment is crucial for building and maintaining a connection with someone. There can't be trust if $L_1$ seems at risk. And you don't need to be a manager to create this kind of space. Allowing others to fully be themselves and let their guard down is the key to creating a safe area—one that can then be occupied while a connection is built.

- You can't pay people to want to become leaders. You know what you create with that type of corporate leadership philosophy? Résumé padders. Folks that want to join programs so they can dive into management and be paid like a manager. If someone is really interested in becoming a leader, give them resources, help, and support so they can be successful. But it's on them whether they put in the work.

- A vice president at my work sent out an email asking us for slogans to help energize the workforce. A "rallying cry" that would boost morale and productivity. Poor executives—they just don't get it. People don't put their heart and soul into their job to build a widget; they do it to support great leaders. When you feel attached and like a valued member of the team, it's incredible how much effort you'll contribute toward the team's goal—something a slickly worded slogan can never do (which is the response I emailed back).

- Always address your team as "we" and not "you" (and certainly never say "I" did something or accomplished something). *We* had an amazing year, not *you* had an amazing year. It sounds like you're not a part of the team this way, and you obviously are, since it's required to be a leader for those people. I get why leaders do this, to deflect praise onto the team, but that usually isn't how it's received. Just say *we* since you're part of the team and its accomplishments.

- Don't let this be your last stop. I dare you to buy another book, watch another talk, take another course. And even if it's not exactly what you were hoping for, one of the best things you can ever do is read something you disagree with. People are weirdly scared to hear ideas they aren't proponents of, but it's not a virus that will consume you. You're allowed to read something and say, "Yeah, that's not for me, I actually don't agree with that." In fact, doing so helps solidify where you stand on a topic. All I'm saying is this: I'm honored you've taken the time to read this book, and I hope it has helped you and your leadership flame be better prepared for stepping out into the world and continuing your leadership journey. But please don't stop here. We as leaders must continue to grow and learn—not only for ourselves, but for those who follow us.

# A Pretty Good Summary

In case you ever want something to quickly reference so you can jog your memory, here is a summary an early reader of the book gave me. I agreed so much with their takeaways that it's been copied verbatim below.

- Anyone can be a leader.
- Leadership is separate from your job/function.
- Leaders have followers, and you have to earn that with every single person on your team daily.
- ■ → ☉ has to be nurtured like a plant.
- Leadership is relative to who you are in the dynamic.
- Leaders are not people pleasers. They must have difficult conversations and make decisions for the team.
- If a person's L1 and L2 aren't being met, they won't choose to follow you.
- There are no set personality traits required to be a good leader.
- Being a leader can at times be hard work, but it will get easier.

# Acknowledgements

Kenzie – The most supportive, patient and caring spouse you could ever ask for. This book was countless hours and years in the making, and I'm 100% certain I couldn't have done it without her.

My Mom and Dad – For too many reasons to list. Thank you for setting the bar so high, and for always putting my needs and wants first.

Bob DeMeyer – It's rare to be exposed to this level of leadership, and thankfully for me it happened during my formative years as a young man. The embodiment of a leader.

Dafna Michaelson Jenet and Michael Jenet – For continually believing in me, and not to mention being the epitome of leadership within our Colorado community.

The rest of my very supportive family, in all the meanings that word can take.

And thank you to the other influential leaders I have had in my life. Everything in this book was shaped by previous experiences, and these individuals played a large part in shaping how I answer – *What is leadership?*

Pat Flynn
Karen Stromme
Bob Nielson
Curt Wiese
Bud Brand

And of course, little Polly.

# ABOUT THE AUTHOR

Joe Reichert is a TEDx speaker, an aerospace program manager, and a leadership coach at a Fortune 500 company. He is a former college football national champion, and one of the youngest head coaches in USARL history. He has created multiple leadership development programs, and holds the record for most executives pissed off in a single meeting. He aspires to make leadership so simple that his services are no longer needed, then live out his days as a hermit with his wife and dog in the mountains, never to open another email again.

# Journey Institute Press

Journey Institute Press is a non-profit publishing house created by authors to flip the publishing model for new authors. Created with intention and purpose to provide the highest quality publishing resources available to authors whose stories might otherwise not be told.

JI Press focusses on women, BIPOC, and LGBTQ+ authors without regard to the genre of their work.

As a Publishing House, our goal is to create a supportive, nurturing, and encouraging environment that puts the author above the publisher in the publishing model.

Journey Ink Publishing is an Imprint of Journey Institute Press, a division of 50 in 52 Journey, Inc.

THE
JOURNEY P
INSTITUTE
P R E S S

www.ingramcontent.com/pod-product-compliance
Lightning Source LLC
Chambersburg PA
CBHW040851210326
41597CB00029B/4803